G M C:

Goal, Motivation, and Conflict

G M C:

Goal, Motivation, and Conflict

The Building Blocks Of Good Fiction

BY
DEBRA DIXON

Gryphon Books for Writers
Memphis, Tennessee

GMC: Goal, Motivation, and Conflict.
 Published by Gryphon Books for Writers, P.O. Box 172342, Memphis, Tennessee 38187. First Edition.

Cover Design by Martha Shields

ISBN 0-9654371-0-8

Table of Contents

INTRODUCTION

IF WRITING WERE EASY, EVERYONE WOULD BE WRITING.

At the beginning of my career, a well-known writer once remarked to me that "We don't like writing. We like *having written.*"

A profound observation.

At least it was for me. I was incredibly relieved to find out that the mega-stars of publishing didn't sit joyfully down at their keyboards and spew forth effortless prose that coalesced into compelling blockbuster novels without the authors ever having had to *work* at it. Nope. They had bad days too. But they kept writing.

Writers write. Period. No matter how hard it is. One word after another. Sometimes the sentences spill quickly from our fingertips and other times we bang our heads against the wall wondering why we do this to ourselves. *"Because you can't NOT write,"* whispers our sneaky, grammatically incorrect subconscious. And so we go back to our masterpiece-in-progress or we start a new story.

With each new project, we become just a little more determined to find an easier way. To avoid our past mistakes. To put the next novel on track and keep it on track.

We go to seminars, workshops, and classes. We buy "how-to" books. We enter contests. We join critique groups and writers' groups. We listen very carefully to what other writers have to say because maybe they've found a shortcut, a magic formula, or the secret of the universe. And sometimes we realize that *we're* the ones who have something to share.

"Goal, motivation, and conflict" was born when my local writers' group asked me to do a program on plotting. I have a vast collection of writing "how-to" and screenwriting books. That's where I learned most of what I know. Almost without exception, each of the books harps (in one way or another) on the concepts of goal, motivation, and conflict. The craft books on my shelves call these three elements by a variety of different names:

Goal—desire, want, need, ambition, purpose

Motivation—drive, backstory, impetus, incentive

Conflict—trouble, tension, friction, villain, roadblock

Regardless of what you call GMC, the bottom line is that these three topics are the foundation of everything that happens in our story world.

And what happens in our story world is called the PLOT. (Yes, that complicated and scary thing called plot can actually be broken down into three elements.) To me, this concept of GMC was simple. Something I had internalized from bits and pieces of more books and workshops than I could count. Yet to the members of my local writers group, GMC was a foreign concept. To my surprise, instead of nodding off in boredom, the writers in my local group sat with mouths open in shock or scribbled notes furiously.

Being the clever creature I am, it wasn't long before I began to suspect that I had discovered something. Not something *new* or incredibly *brilliant*, just something *understandable*. In the quest for the secret of the universe, writers want something which can be applied to our own work. Something we can internalize and utilize.

After giving that first workshop on GMC, I found that I was using GMC in a variety of ways beyond plotting. I use the concept for character development, sharpening scenes, fixing sagging middles, creating memorable secondary characters, writing synopses, pitching ideas to my editor, and evaluating whether an idea is going to work before I've written two hundred pages. GMC seems to be a part of my thought process—an unconscious filter I apply to my work.

After having taught the concept in my university course as well as around the country, I've seen that GMC can be valuable for almost every type of writer. Some use GMC in "prepping" the book or "pre-writing." Other writers just write the book by the seat of their pants and then use GMC during their revision process. Still others use GMC only when preparing for an editor interview or composing query letters.

Every writer is unique. Each writer's process of writing is unique. There is no right or wrong way to approach your manuscript, story idea, or revision. Seek first to understand the concept of GMC, and only then ask yourself how you can use GMC in your own work.

To help you understand GMC, I'm going to pick it apart—letter by letter. Goal. Motivation. Conflict. By the time you've finished this book, those words will be burned into your brain. You'll never be able to watch a movie again without thinking of them. And your reading is going to suffer too. Once you become aware of GMC, you'll find it's *everywhere!*

And speaking of movies...

You have your first assignment. Go rent and watch the following movies.

The Wizard of Oz (absolute necessity)
Ladyhawke
The Client
Star Wars
Casablanca
The Fugitive

Why am I asking you to watch movies instead of asking you to read books? Because people's reading tastes vary too much. Movies are visual. Movies can't "tell" you anything. Movies have to show you. Movies can't bog you down with exposition, narrative, or description. Film is a quick, accessible medium. And most people can watch six movies more easily than they can read six books.

One word of caution: Even if you have already seen these movies, please rent and view them again. Little details are important. Especially watch ***The Wizard of Oz***. This movie is the backbone of our exploration of GMC. There is a very good reason that this movie became a classic, and that reason is goal, motivation, and conflict.

Chapter One

WHO, WHAT, WHY, AND WHY NOT

These are the important questions for any story. Your job as a writer is to answer them quickly and clearly. The benefit to doing your job is the satisfaction of knowing that you're hooking the reader. Once you've got the reader hooked, you want the reader to continue turning those pages.

For most writers, that first reader is an editor or an agent. Both are jaded creatures, tired of turning pages. The size of the "slush" piles of unsolicited manuscripts in New York would give you a heart attack. In some publishing houses and agencies, slush piles—three feet high—literally line office walls. Then you have to add the piles of *solicited* or requested manuscripts and partial manuscripts.

Before you become depressed, I should tell you that every editor I have ever met *wants* to discover someone new and wonderful in that pile of manuscripts. Editors and agents are book lovers. They are also industry professionals, which means they have high standards and high expectations. If you want to publish your work, then you've got to get their attention.

Editors and agents are a little like Clint Eastwood. No, they don't grab a manuscript and utter, "Make my day." But you can bet they're thinking, "Make me care." Flashy metaphors and proper sentence structure aren't going to do it. You need a strong foundation. You need compelling characters.

That's what *all* readers want when they sit down with a book. They want the writer to make them care.

So how do you do that? How do you make readers care? You give them something fresh. You give them unique, well-rounded characters with goals and motivations.

If you push cardboard characters through a tired and predictable series of events, you'll end up with a generic book **and** a generic rejection from a publishing house. Instead of handy stereotypes like dumb blondes, macho jocks, and spoiled little rich girls, give readers someone who walks off the page and into their emotions. Give the reader someone to agree or disagree with. Give the reader someone who is in a world of trouble with no way out.

Consider Jo from Louisa May Alcott's book ***Little Women***. Jo is much more than a stereotypical tomboy. She has a sensitive side, writes passionate fiction, and isn't afraid to show tenderness to those she loves. She even has a maternal streak that peaks out from time to time. In fact, being a tomboy is only one facet of Jo's complex personality.

There are no new plots, but there are plenty of fresh new characters with which you can grab the reader. Characterization is the key to successful commercial fiction. Characterization starts with goal, motivation, and conflict.

Character is the who of "who, what, why, and why not."

Remember those important questions? The ones that you have to answer right up front in order to grab your reader?

Spend time developing your characters beyond the physical aspects. Answer that important question—**who is this book about?** Some writers fill out character questionnaires with information such as hobbies, relatives, achievements, etc. Some writers prefer to write character sketches or mini-biographies as a way to understand their characters.

I use a role-playing technique called the character interview. My critique partners interview me as though I were my character. First, I tell them a little bit about my character and then the grilling begins. A typical interview lasts forty-five minutes to an hour. There is no pre-determined list of questions, and I always use a tape recorder so that I don't have to waste time taking notes.

Questions can be as simple as "What's your favorite color?" and as complex as "Who has disappointed you the most and why?" The interviews usually take unexpected twists and turns like this exchange.

> *"Did you go to your prom?"*
> *"No."*
> *"Why?"*
> *"I don't like crowds."*
> *"Why?"*
> *"Because I can feel the emotions of the people around me."*

From this I discovered that my archaeologist was also empathic. Surprise! Surprise! The possibility might never have occurred to me if I hadn't utilized the character interview process. This character's empathic ability became a critical element of conflict between my hero and heroine in ***Mountain Mystic***.

No matter which method you choose, the reward is well worth it. If you can trace every action in your book to a unique character's goal and motivation, then the character will create the plot right before your eyes. The plot will be inevitable, because your protagonist (or main character, also referred to as "hero" in this book) will have an "agenda" that drives him or her. The character will make decisions that turn the book in new directions.

Most importantly the character will compel your reader to turn the page by ushering the reader through the story. And speaking of ushering, let me caution you to go easy on the number of characters you introduce in the first ten to twenty pages of your book. Certainly many of you are writing books that have several important characters. Most books have a minimum of two important story people—the hero/heroine and the villain. And some writers naturally gravitate to complicated stories with a multitude of characters.

But be careful of introducing a cast of thousands. Nothing will make the reader put down your book faster than a disjointed, confusing first chapter. And nothing can kill your chance to capture the reader more quickly than a flat first chapter—a chapter that is bogged down with too much character history or backstory.

First chapters are like a first impression—you only get one chance. **So don't blow it.**

As Dwight Swain says in *Techniques of the Selling Writer*, "...let your readers know there's going to be a fight...and it's the kind of fight that will interest [them]." Swain is absolutely right about this point. As a writer you want your reader to identify with the character and situation. You want your reader to understand what your book is going to be about.

Don't you hate missing the first few minutes of a movie? That's because in those first few minutes, the movie will establish who, what, why, and why not. When you miss those critical moments, you may feel a step behind. Outside the circle. Left out of the joke. And cranky.

The first chapter of a book performs the same function as those first minutes in a movie. The first chapter must establish what's at stake and make an introduction. You are introducing the reader to their guides for the evening—the hero, villain, and maybe even one or two other characters. (Note: Your story hero may be a male or female.)

Keep in mind that the reader is supposed to *identify* and *empathize* with your character from the moment the character makes an entrance. (If the first character you introduce is clearly a villain, you still must engage and fascinate the reader. But for the moment I am going to assume your first character is going to be the protagonist.) You want to "fix" that important character in the reader's mind. And you don't want to waste time doing it.

Your reader wants to become involved in the character's struggle to achieve a specific **goal**. The reader wants to understand why your character is **motivated** to achieve that goal. And the reader wants to "worry" about whether or not the character can actually achieve that goal. **Conflict** creates the worry.

If the hero has a wonderful life and everything he wants, then your book is going to be boring. An editor won't buy the book. Readers won't pick it up. And if they do, they won't finish it. Because you will not have met their expectations of being taken on a journey of uncertainty.

What we are talking about are the expectations of commercial fiction readers. Someone buying a literary work focusing on one aspect of a character's life or someone buying experimental fiction, or even someone buying a biography may expect slower pacing. Less dialogue. More exposition or description. (Please note: I am not saying that all literary titles or biographies are slower, speechless and flowery! No. I'm simply saying that different forms of fiction carry different reader expectations. What a writer might try in experimental fiction, just won't fly with the mass audience in commercial fiction.)

Commercial fiction readers expect your characters to have goals, to be motivated, and to face conflict. They expect you to answer four simple questions.

Who	=	character
What	=	goal
Why	=	motivation
Why not	=	conflict

Why am I harping on these questions?

These elements all work together in your book. We've all heard the saying that no man is an island. Well, none of these "W" words is an island either. They are linked so firmly together that they form a complete sentence when put together correctly. Here's how it works:

> *A character wants a goal because he is motivated, but he faces conflict.*

See what a neat package these elements make? But this sentence is generic. To see the real power of the relationship of these elements, let's look at something specific:

> *An unhappy teenager wants to get home to Kansas because her aunt is sick, but first she must fight a witch to win the aid of the wizard who has the power to send her home.*

Another way of conveying the same information, but in a shorter version, would be:

> *A tornado blows Dorothy to a magic land where she must fight a witch and seek the wizard who has the power to send her home to her sick aunt.*

Either version gives you a good idea of the story concept. Both versions were created using the W's. Knowing the **who, what, why, and why not** of your story will give you a handle on the idea. How you actually express that information isn't the issue. What *is* key is that you understand that "who, what, why, and why not" are important questions to readers and to editors. They want answers. Editors especially need information that is clear, concise, and helps them to understand your work.

Wrapping up

In this chapter I've introduced the W's to you and discussed the importance of the first W— the "who" of your book and why GMC is so important to creating character. In the next few chapters I'll examine the WHAT, the WHY, and the WHY NOT. That's goal, motivation, and conflict.

Chapter Two

GOAL: WHAT YOUR CHARACTER WANTS

A goal is a desired result, a purpose or an objective. A goal is the prize or reward that your character wants to obtain or achieve. Everybody likes a winner, and readers are no exception to that rule.

Readers want to see a character overcome obstacles. They want to live vicariously through the character in your book, feeling every setback. Feeling the conflict. And getting the satisfaction of accomplishment when the character finally reaches his goal.

In order for the reader to immerse himself in the character's struggles, first the reader has to clearly understand your character's goal. It's your job as the author to identify your character's goal and then to point your character toward that goal. If you aim the character, the reader will follow. Happily.

So what makes a good goal?

Characters should want what they don't have yet. Characters who simply want more of what they *already* have are not strong characters. In fact, story people should desperately *need* what they don't have yet. Dangle a carrot just out of their reach and make sure they haven't had a bite to eat in weeks. Then that carrot becomes important. The carrot becomes something your character desperately needs.

In real life everybody wants something. Everybody's got an agenda. That's what makes life so unpredictable, and this can work for you in fiction as well. Characters who want something—who desperately need something—won't sit around like bumps on logs. They'll go after their goal. They'll take action.

Action is important.

Active characters will make your life much easier because action creates plot. And, frankly, you need a plot if you're going to write a book, so why not let your characters create it for you? Let them slug their way through the book toward their goal. The havoc they wreak makes excellent reading.

The best goals are important and urgent.

Goals should be important enough for the character to act against his own best interest and to endure hardship if necessary. "Important enough" means that there will be unpleasant consequences if the goal is not achieved. People will move heaven and earth to avoid unpleasant consequences. It's a fact of human nature.

Let's define exactly what constitutes something "unpleasant." Unpleasant could mean mortifying or embarrassing (comedy). Unpleasant could represent something fatal or dangerous (suspense, thrillers, mysteries). It could be a heartbreaking event (tear-jerker). Unpleasant could be that the character will enter a desperate financial situation such as bankruptcy. Falling in love can even be an unpleasant consequence if the character wants to avoid love.

Regardless of what the unpleasant consequence is, it's usually found wrapped up in the motivation, which I'll talk about in the next chapter. For now just focus on the fact that goals should be important. Failure for your character means facing the consequence.

A sense of urgency is also vital for fictional goals. It hooks the editor and hooks the reader. If your hero or heroine's action toward the goal can be postponed until next year or even next week then you need a new goal!

Why? You lose urgency if the characters don't need to take action *now*. Without a sense of urgency, why should the editor read your story now? She can read your story next year just as easily as tonight because it's not urgent and gripping. There will be nothing to make her act *now,* unless your story concept/query makes her want to grab the manuscript and start that first paragraph. Then, you want her to finish the paragraph, turn the page, and keep turning.

A sense of urgency will set your book apart from the hundreds of manuscripts editors see that are nice stories going nowhere. Remember editors pick up a manuscript and think, "Make me care." You want something urgent. Something important. That's why "deadline" stories are so popular.

Give a retired burglar three days to steal the Hope diamond or his sister will be killed. Give a mother, who's fighting for custody, a job opportunity that will never come again. Ask a computer hacker to find a way into the government computer that has erroneously marked him for termination with extreme prejudice. Give a reluctant single woman five days to create the perfect Christmas season for a little boy who's not sure anyone loves him enough to keep him.

All of the above examples present a character with a situation requiring action. Someone has to do something. *Now.*

Urgency need not be a time constraint. Your story doesn't have to have a calendar or clock deadline to be effective. Urgent is simply something requiring immediate attention. People make unusual decisions under pressure. Some decisions lead to humor, some to danger, some to mistakes.

All you need to make the unpredictable happen is the sense of urgency attached to your character's goals. In other words, goals should feel crucial and add tension to your story. Urgency should push your character forward. When the character feels time running out or opportunity's door closing, he's got to make a decision. And he's got to make it quick.

Remember I said earlier, that you should give your reader a character to agree or disagree with. The simplest way to do that is to push your character to the wall and have him take action. The reader can then agree or disagree with the character's decision. Either way you're a winner, because the reader will turn those pages to see what happens.

Goals are not always achieved.

Yes, in some stories the characters don't reach their goals. But novels in which the goal is not achieved usually aren't as satisfying to readers as stories with closure. As an example of a story in which the goal is not achieved, consider a plot revolving around a cop, whose objective/goal is to catch a killer. Three-hundred pages later (and you know it's the end because you're running out of pages in the book), the cop knocks on the door of the killer's house. The killer spies the cop, runs out the back door, and roars off in a van, escaping justice.

Would you be satisfied?

No. Neither would I. That's the kind of book that leaves a dent in my wall because I tend to get violent when my expectations aren't met. When I've slogged my way through three-hundred and fifty pages of a book, I want some satisfaction. This story would not have given me closure. (Completely tidy endings are not necessary either. I'll get to that in a moment.)

What if the killer roars off, *but* leaves behind all the evidence the cop needs to finally prove the killer's true identity?

Okay, that's a better conclusion, but the bottom line is that the cop still did not *catch* the killer. The killer got away. End of story. Literally.

Since we're talking about mass market *commercial* fiction, this is not the type of story I would recommend to new writers. This type of story violates reader trust. Your contract with the reader is that you will entertain. You will not cheat. And you will deliver the goods.

In the case of the cop's story, were the goods delivered? That depends. If the goal for the character, *as developed by the author,* was to catch the killer, then NO! On the other hand, if the cop had two goals: **one**—to catch the killer, and **two**—to clear his own name of suspicion, then the story can be seen as having delivered the goods. The cop did clear his name. He would have reached one of his goals.

Would that make me happy? Not completely. I would still have felt cheated.

"But what if the book had a sequel where the cop goes after the killer again?" Bingo. The story *could* be structured for a sequel, with the apprehension of the killer the focus of book number two.

The key to satisfying the reader is understanding that you are writing a book that requires a sequel. Once you understand that the book has a larger scope, you can structure the novel so that your character struggles and achieves partial success. You can complete your contract with the reader so that the reader trusts you enough to buy the sequel.

Goals in a romance novel

Excuse me while I climb on a soapbox. The heroine's goal in a romance novel is ***not*** to fall in love and get married. Ditto for the hero. The last thing on their minds is meeting a soul mate. In fact, it's darned inconvenient. Romance will be a conflict for your characters. Otherwise, they'd run toward each other on page one, kiss, fall into bed, and get married.

That makes a very short book.

When you are working with goals think about how a romance will complicate matters. I wrote a book about an arson investigator and a pyromaniac—one wanted to solve a crime and the other wanted to clear her name. Falling in love made achieving their goals more difficult.

If you write a romance in which the hero and heroine wander from date to date, the reader will soon be bored. Where's the struggle? Who are we rooting for? What are the consequences? What's at stake?

Suspense works well in many romances, but suspense is not the only way to create strong goals for characters. All that is required is that the character care about their goals. Shipwreck a single mother on an island. Your heroine will be focused on getting back to her daughter. She's got no time for a tropical romance.

Pit a well-known psychic against a hero sworn to debunk her. Your heroine wants to prove she's the genuine article. The hero will be trying like hell to trip her up. What will she do to prove herself? What happens when the hero finds himself wanting to believe the heroine might be a real psychic?

Falling in love should impact the characters original goals. Falling in love should require your hero and heroine to make choices.

Always throw the reader a bone.

Reader trust is very important. If you've delivered the goods once, then you can probably deliver them a second time. And a third. And a fourth...etc. Readers who trust you will buy your books forever. They will be loyal. Nothing helps a career more than your *first* reader—the editor.

So my advice to new writers is to have the character achieve his goal. *Throw them a bone.* If it's a romance, then have the characters actually fall in love and make a commitment. Make sure the hero and heroine are still alive at the end of the book. Give the romance reader the happily-ever-after he/she expects!

If you're writing a cozy mystery, you have to solve the crime. Your detective must ferret out all the clues and nab the bad guy. Never forget that you have a contract with your reader.

But what if my character's goal changes during the course of the book? Is that cheating the reader?

Not to worry. This is not a bad thing. Goals do sometimes change. Let's take the case of the cop trying to catch a killer. The one who suddenly finds himself framed for the murders.

Well...finding the killer takes a back seat to the cop clearing his own name. Prison is no place to be if you're a cop. This subtle shifting of goals from civic duty to personal crisis ups the ante.

Many writers instinctively create goal changes which turn up the heat in their books. They get to "the end" and are surprised to find that the goal they began with was not the goal the character achieved. That's okay! Just make certain if your character changes goals that his reasons are clear to the reader.

Good old-fashioned common sense is indispensable. Is the shift reasonable? Is it logical? Can you show the reader why your character's priorities have changed? Are you keeping the goal changes to a minimum?

Nothing is more irritating than a character who wanders around changing his mind about what's important every five minutes. You'll have your reader yelling, "What's the point?" and tossing the book at the wall if you do that.

A good rule for beginning writers is "one character, one goal."

This GMC thing seems full of rules! Do this! Don't do that! What's the deal?

Let me digress from GMC just a moment to remind you that for every rule there is a writer talented enough to do the exact opposite and make believers of us all. What I am sharing are suggestions to help you avoid some of the pitfalls waiting to suck your work into the quicksand of rejection.

Writing craft guidelines are not stone tables from the mountain. Every writer has a different style. Feel free to have your character change his mind a thousand times about his goal as long as you understand why you are doing it. Understand the craft of writing, and then make it work for you.

As an example of making the craft work for me, I regularly

alternate viewpoint within scenes. A lot. To many writers this is heresy. However, I don't happen to subscribe to the particular doctrine/rule that says, "Thou shall have only one point of view per scene."

That doesn't work for my style. So I studied viewpoint, studied writers who alternated viewpoint within scenes, learned how they handled the switches. Once I knew the mechanics of viewpoint, I felt free to break the rules for *specific* reasons in my own writing. GMC helps me understand which character has the most at stake and knowing that, I also know when to change viewpoint.

A good rule of thumb (yes, another rule) is to experiment with the craft. Follow the rules. Then break the rules if necessary. Find out what works for you and use it. What works for me is to change viewpoint characters when the emotional weight of the scene changes. See? I have a consistent rule to follow, but it's one I developed after studying the issue.

You can't go wrong with urgency.

Now back to those slippery goals that change on you when you least expect it. Your greatest concern when changing your character's goals is that you don't lose the urgency you've worked so hard to build. In the case of the cop, finding a killer before he kills again is a pretty urgent goal. But his new goal of clearing his name increases the pressure to find the killer because the cop now has a personal stake in the investigation. Time is running out and he's about to be arrested.

In many romances, it is the escalating romance that provides the sense of urgency. Sexual tension fuels the characters determination to achieve their goal and get the heck out of Dodge before they lose their hearts.

Give a gentleman pirate access to a woman who might know the location of a buried treasure and give a rival buccaneer part of a map. Now it's a race. Can the buccaneer decipher the map before the pirate breaks the woman?

Urgent. Urgent. Urgent.

You couldn't find a better slogan to help you with goals.

Filling in the blanks

Before we go farther, here's an example of a chart that I'll be using throughout the course of this book as we build the GMC for Dorothy in the *Wizard of Oz*. And, yes, I really do use the chart in my own work.

Character	EXTERNAL	INTERNAL
Goal		
Motivation		
Conflict		

Make your chart using an 8 1/2" x 11" (landscape/sideways) sheet of paper. This size lets you use small sticky notes while you're filling in each box. In the beginning stages of any fiction book, the GMC chart takes a lot of abuse, cursing, and erasing. With sticky notes it's much easier to change elements that don't work or aren't strong enough to suit you. Sticky notes are easy to pull off and replace or even to move to another square altogether.

Some authors have told me they use a poster board with large sticky notes for GMC charts. Others use a dry/erase board. Still others use the computer because they can't think "on paper." Some keep it in their head or use a pencil and notebook paper.

No matter how you keep track of your GMC after you've become familiar with the concept, it's a good idea to use the charts in the beginning—when you're still grappling with the individual elements and how they relate to one another.

Especially helpful is placing GMC charts of your central characters side by side to see how their GMC's overlap to create echoes and generate conflict. If your main characters' GMC charts *don't* clash with each other, then you have to ask yourself why are these people in your book? Are they allies or enemies? Are they both? And if the charts show they are neither, you'd better go back and do some work! You want your characters to feed off each other, to push each other forward, to create roadblocks.

Creating a great read is a lot like throwing a pack of snarling dogs into one cage and then waiting to see who wins. Make sure your main character's goal puts him in conflict with other characters. What does he want from these other story people? What do they want from him?

Remember goal is all about what your characters want. Everybody has an agenda.

Goals for the *Wizard of Oz*

Dorothy has one big overriding goal in the *Wizard of Oz*. What does she want? She wants to get home to Kansas.

Her goal is simple—get home. It's clear. It's very easy to

understand. It's not subtle. Goals *should not* be subtle. Get out the two by four and start whacking your reader over the head. "This is what my character wants." Whack. Whack. Whack.

For Dorothy, the goal may be simple but the path to achieving her goal is more difficult. Getting home provides her with several smaller goals that must all be achieved in order to reach her ultimate goal of getting home.

First, she has to get to the Emerald City. Second, she has to get in to see the Wizard. Third, she has to secure the Witch's broomstick.

She's got to do all of these things before she's in a position to get herself home. There are very good reasons that she must accomplish all of these things. That's motivation, which will get into in the next chapter. For now, here's what Dorothy's GMC chart looks like.

Dorothy	EXTERNAL	INTERNAL
Goal	GET HOME 1 Get to Emerald City 2 See the Wizard 3 Get the broomstick	
Motivation		
Conflict		

You'll notice that I've only filled in the information for Dorothy's external goal, which can also be referred to as the "outer goal." An external goal has nothing to do with emotional needs, spirituality, or life's lessons. You can see very easily that "getting home" has nothing to do with Dorothy's emotions or the internal landscape of the character.

If you can see it, touch it, taste it, hear it, or smell it...that's external. Getting home is physical and therefore external. If the character has to feel it (experience emotion), then you're dealing with the internal side of your character.

Dorothy's character goes beyond the external plot, and this gives her depth. Internally, what Dorothy is looking for is her heart's desire. Keep in mind that we are dealing with a teenager and every teenager on the face of the earth is looking for what's going to make them happy and satisfy them emotionally.

Because Dorothy has both inner and outer (internal and external) GMC, she is multi-layered. She doesn't just want to get home to Kansas. She's also on the lookout for her heart's desire. She has an emotional component working hand-in-hand with the external plot.

This combination of inner and outer GMC is found in every character with whom I've ever fallen in love. If you take a look at your keeper shelf, you'll probably find the central characters in those books had strong GMC. In fact you'll probably find that all the characters had strong GMC, which leads me to my next point.

Every character in your book who isn't a walk-on unnamed sack boy should have GMC. The GMC may not be on the finished written page because the character may be a minor character, a non-viewpoint character to whom you can't give much page space. But *you* must know what every character's GMC is. You should know what is driving the story people in your book.

If everyone in your book has an agenda, then all the characters are players. And when your people are players, things happen. Your scenes suddenly jump off the page. They crackle with life because the reader doesn't know what's going to happen. Everybody wants something, and they're angling to get it. The reader doesn't know who's going to win.

Giving a character internal and external goals helps you keep the pressure on. Dorothy's chart now looks like this.

Dorothy	EXTERNAL	INTERNAL
Goal	GET HOME 1 Get to Emerald City 2 See the Wizard 3 Get the broomstick	To find her heart's desire and a place with no trouble.
Motivation		
Conflict		

You can run but you can't hide from goals.

Harrison Ford made a great Richard Kimball in the remake of *The Fugitive.* Only part of the movie can be attributed to the popularity of the actors. The strong story, vivid scenes, and pacing contributed just as much. Where do you think all that good stuff came from? Each character had great GMC.

Kimball wants to find the man who killed his wife. This external goal is urgent. Best of all, this goal is important enough for Kimball to act against his own best interest. Finding his wife's killer is so important that he becomes a fugitive rather than give up the chance. So important that he jumps out of a drainage pipe, falling hundreds of feet into a churning river. He chooses to face death rather than pass up the chance to fight back.

Character decisions create your plot.

This is a clear example of a character making a decision under pressure. Kimball was damned if he did and damned if he didn't. But he acted, and because he acted we couldn't wait to see how his decision turned out. His decision drew us further into the movie. We invested ourselves in his struggle.

Now for Kimball's internal goal. This is a hard one because the film is largely silent on the internal GMC, leaving the audience to infer the obvious internal goal. Kimball wants to stop feeling guilty for being too late to save his wife, too weak to stop her murderer. He wants to do something to make up for his failure.

Other characters in *The Fugitive* had strong external GMC as well. Deputy Marshal Samuel Gerard wants to apprehend the fugitive Richard Kimball. Gerard thinks he's got a dangerous man on the loose. Kimball is a convicted murderer. Gerard's reputation is on the line, and he pulls out all the stops to bring his quarry to justice.

Dr. Charlie Nichols' goal is to keep Kimball away from the marshals, to keep him isolated. Nichols wants to keep Kimball from discovering the truth of his wife's death because Nichols is responsible for her murder.

The son of Kimball's landlord is arrested for selling drugs, and his goal is to reduce the charges against him. He can do this by giving Kimball's location to the cops if they'll drop the charges.

Baby steps toward larger goals

Finding the man who killed Kimball's wife isn't a piece of cake for our hero. He must first accomplish several small but urgent goals, just as Dorothy had to work toward her goal of getting home to Kansas. The first smaller goal for Kimball is to put some distance between himself and the law. He's got to get away. Then he needs clothes, a change of appearance. He needs to tend his wound.

Once all that's done, he must find a way to get access to the hospital so he can check the prosthetics records and put together a list of suspects for his one-armed man. He must track down each of them. He's got to get in and out of the jail where one of the men on his list is being held.

Whew! Richard Kimball is a busy man, which creates a fast paced plot. All of his smaller goals lead him closer to his big goal. Each obstacle teaches him something and leads him closer to the truth.

Smaller goals should help you build to your climax. Smaller goals should change the characters by giving them more confidence or instilling doubt. Smaller goals should create consequences which drive your plot. In *The Fugitive* Kimball's goal of checking his list of suspects leads him to the jail, which places him squarely in the enemy camp—the law. This is dangerous. The scene creates tension and shows us how committed Kimball is to his mission.

Multiple external goals are okay too.

Some characters will want several things simultaneously. A word of caution though. Make sure the character's goals feed off each other or you'll find yourself wrestling with a book going in two separate directions. Consider Luke Skywalker of *Star Wars*. He wants to be a Jedi Knight. *AND* he wants to locate and help the Princess he saw in the R2D2 hologram. Two strong "big picture" goals.

They feed off each other. Learning the ways of the Jedi

Knight is imperative to his helping the Princess and blowing away the Death Star. His quest to help the Princess leads him to the man who can train him as a Jedi. These two separate goals mesh to push the story forward.

Multiple goals are like meteors. They should crash into each other.

Play it again, Sam.

Casablanca provides a strong example of a character with two goals. Rick Blaine doesn't believe in much of anything. Times are dangerous. The world's at war. All he cares about, all he *wants* is to keep his bar from being closed down. That's his first goal—keeping his bar open.

And then in walks his past—Ilsa Lund-Laslow. Rick wants to punish Ilsa for leaving him in Paris. But then his goal changes as he realizes the danger to Ilsa and Victor. Helping her could jeopardize his business, could jeopardize goal number one. Now he's got to walk a tightrope as he takes on a second external goal—to get Ilsa on that plane.

Internally poor old Rick is also in bad shape. He'd like to regain the love that he had in Paris with Ilsa. But he also wants to do what's right for the world. Getting Ilsa and her husband, who is important to the war effort, on that plane and out of harm's way is what's right for the world.

Rick's multiple goals constantly force him to make decisions. Tough decisions.

It's hard to believe that this great classic movie was written "brainstorm style." Each night they'd write the scenes for the next day. The writers created strong characters and put them in tough situations. They put snarling dogs in a box and waited to see what happened. It worked because the characters had strong goals, motivations, and conflicts.

Wrapping up

There you have it. Goal. The first important element of GMC. Goals come in all shapes and sizes. The goal is your character's call to adventure. The goal is why the character takes action.

Important points to remember:

1. Goals must be important and urgent. Failure will create consequences for the character.

2. Multi-layered characters have both external and internal goals.

3. The large central goal of a character is often accompanied by a series of smaller goals which drive the action of the book.

4. Characters goals can change over the course of a book.

5. All the characters in your book should have GMC.

6. Character decisions drive the plot.

7. Goals are not always achieved by the characters. But if you choose this structure, you must satisfy the reader in other ways.

8. Multiple goals are like meteors. They should crash into each other and have impact on your character—forcing him to make decisions.

Chapter Three

MOTIVATION: "THE WHY"

Goal was the "what." Motivation is the "why." Why do your characters want this? Why do they have to reach their goal? Why? Why? Why? Such a tiny word for such an essential element of fiction.

Motivation is what drives your character to obtain or achieve his goal. Story people can have several motivations, all pointing to the same goal. However first time authors should give their characters one good strong motivation.

Keep it simple. Keep it strong. Keep it focused.

Jugglers don't begin to juggle by trying to keep five balls in the air. Of course not. Juggling is a difficult skill to learn. So is writing. Both skills should be taken one step at a time.

Anyone can toss balls in the air, just as anyone can put words on a page. The true test is what happens once those balls are airborne. Or once those words are read by someone other than the writer.

Writing is communication. If you fail to sufficiently motivate your characters, your confused reader will frown and draw his brows together. He will shake his head and roll his eyes. If you fail to answer the question "why?" your fickle reader will scoff at your efforts. He will not be able to suspend his disbelief long enough to immerse himself in your story world. He won't believe in your characters.

You will have failed to communicate.

Motivation is possibly the most important of the three elements of GMC because you can do anything in fiction. There are *no* limits. Everything truly is possible as long as you help your reader understand *why* your characters do what they do. *Why* they land themselves in impossible situations. *Why* they make the choices they make.

Think of motivation as the magic that helps the reader empathize with your character.

Motivation is often preceded by the word "because." When you see that word, you know an explanation is coming. "Because" is the trigger for a motivation clause. Why did the chicken cross the road? *Because* it wanted to get to the other side.

*The character wants a goal **because** he is motivated.*

Dorothy wants to get home to Kansas *because*...why?

Simple. She has to get home to Kansas *because* her Auntie Em is sick. We aren't left to guess or assume what makes Dorothy tick. The filmmaker beautifully sets up the motivation in the black and white portion of the movie.

Dorothy has run away from home *because* everything in her life is horrible. (Notice the "because" in the previous sentence. The clause reveals *why* Dorothy ran away in the first place. "Because" and "why" are linked. If you have one, you have the other.) Okay, so Dorothy's run away. She meets a fortune teller who's more of a scam artist than a fortune teller, but he's a good man at heart. He sees the basket and correctly guesses she's run away from home. He has her close her eyes so that he can tell her future and send her home where she belongs.

While Dorothy has her eyes closed, he busily rummages around in her bags to find clues so he can sound brilliant. When he finds the picture of Auntie Em, he wonders aloud if there is an older woman in her life. Poor Dorothy is buying the psychic bit hook, line, and sinker. So the fortune teller closes the deal by mumbling about Auntie Em clutching her heart, wondering if she could be sick, *planting the idea* in Dorothy's mind that Auntie Em needs her.

Needs her now. Pronto. There's no time to waste.

Once again we are back to the issue of urgency. Urgency always pushes the plot and the pace.

Upon hearing the bad news about Auntie Em, Dorothy is out of the fortune teller's wagon like a shot. She rushes through the middle of a tornado to get home *because* she *believes* her aunt is sick and may die without her help. This is the same motivation that drives Dorothy once she reaches the Land of Oz.

Oz is a wonderful place with munchkins, has a beautiful landscape and exciting magical properties. Ordinarily a person might stay for a while, explore Oz, take a two or three week vacation and *then* worry about getting home. But not Dorothy. She has a sense of urgency. Auntie Em is going to keel over dead if she doesn't get home.

That is a strong enough motivation to make Dorothy do whatever it takes, act against her own best interest in order to get home to Kansas. Dorothy will risk anything, put everything on the line so she can get to Auntie Em. Our teenaged character has a solid reason for her actions.

We've just filled in the external motivation blank on Dorothy's GMC chart.

Dorothy	EXTERNAL	INTERNAL
Goal	GET HOME 1 Get to Emerald City 2 See the Wizard 3 Get the broomstick	To find her heart's desire and a place with no trouble.
Motivation	AUNTIE EM IS SICK	
Conflict		

Nurture the little goals too. Lay a foundation for all your scenes.

Motivating your characters for the larger goals is not enough. You must create compelling reasons for every action in your book. In *The Wizard of Oz* Dorothy has the three smaller goals listed on the chart. Each of them is as strongly motivated as her larger goal. Solving the problem of getting home forces her to make decisions and take action. She must reach each of these smaller goals or she won't make it home.

You'll notice in the following question/answer structure, which explains the motivation for the smaller goals, each of the answers begins with "because." Remember when you are trying to put your own GMC into a single sentence, "because" is the trigger for motivation.

> Why does Dorothy need to get to the Emerald City?
> *Because the Wizard is there.*
>
> Why does Dorothy need to get in to see the Wizard?
> *Because she's been told by the Good Witch that the Wizard has the power to send her home.*
>
> Why does Dorothy need the broomstick of the Wicked Witch?
> *Because the Wizard wants the broomstick as his payment for sending her home.*

Whoa. Time out. Let's think about this logically. Dorothy, a teenaged outsider with no skills, is going to attempt to steal the broomstick of the Wicked Witch, who has magical powers? Not only is Dorothy going to steal the broom, but she must go to the Witch's castle to get it?

"No one in their right mind would try that!"

True enough. So how is the filmmaker going to make the reader believe this plot twist? With motivation. It's moments like this which make GMC such a indispensable trick of the trade. An unmotivated character would simply walk away from the Wizard's challenge, throw up her hands, and say, "I'm done."

If Auntie Em simply had a common cold or sinus infection,

this plot wouldn't work. But Auntie Em doesn't have a cold, and Dorothy can't walk away. Her one overriding motivation provides all the fuel we require to keep the story going. Auntie Em needs her. Auntie Em was clutching her heart and might die, so Dorothy will act against her own best interest to take on this task.

Dorothy will walk into danger because she has no other choice. And the reader is going to follow her because we understand her urgency. We understand why she thinks she has to get back to Auntie Em. We're rooting for her, and we're worried about her.

If you provide a strong enough motivation, your reader will follow you (and your characters) anywhere—into alien spaceships, through time travel warps, along with little old ladies who take on the mafia by themselves. The key is proper motivation.

Setting yourself up for success

One author told me that before she was published she kept giving her protagonists real life motivations. She also kept getting rejected despite her unprecedented recognition in national contests for unpublished writers. So she stepped back and took a hard look at her work. What she found surprised her.

Her characters had ordinary, garden-variety motivations, which weren't strong enough. Certainly the motivations were "real" but they simply weren't strong enough. When she replaced normal motivation with larger-than-life motivation, she sold her first book. And many more since then.

Larger-than-life motivation doesn't mean your hero flies around in a Superman cape to save the world. Larger-than-life simply means important.

An example would be a heroine who wants to disappear, to

hide from an abusive husband. Her motivation is to protect her child. That motivation is clear, important, and impossible to miss. Any reader can empathize and understand why the heroine is driven to disappear. A much weaker story, one with a garden-variety motivation, would be the story of a woman who wants to disappear because she's lost her boss's tax return and misfiled all his expense reports. Unless her boss is a mafia godfather, this heroine doesn't have much motivation for disappearing.

Proper motivation is the missing component for many authors. In fiction we have to have our characters do things they wouldn't normally do. To pull off this hat-trick, our characters have to be well motivated. Like Dorothy.

You can't give your character an opportunity to back away from the story. Throw him out into the storm and slam the door behind him. Bolt it if you have to. Just don't let your character turn away from the challenge.

The Wizard of Oz wouldn't be as effective a story if Dorothy was worried about her undone chores or worried about being yelled at for missing dinner. The story works because Dorothy is worried about her family, about Auntie Em specifically. None of us will ever know if the filmmaker considered a screen adaptation in which Dorothy worried about her chores, but I'm betting he didn't. At least not for very long.

Using the chart to analyze your story potential

What might sound plausible in theory doesn't always work in the cold black and white reality of the written page or on the screen. Using the GMC chart you can visualize where your story is going. You can assess whether the motivation is strong enough to compel your characters to take on the challenges you have in store for them.

Take a look at Dorothy's updated GMC chart. The integral relationship between the external goal and motivation is clear.

Dorothy	EXTERNAL	INTERNAL
Goal	GET HOME 1 Get to Emerald City 2 See the Wizard 3 Get the broomstick	To find her heart's desire and a place with no trouble.
Motivation	AUNTIE EM IS SICK 1 The Wizard is there. 2 He has the power to send her home. 3 The price for sending her home.	
Conflict		

Motivation pushes Dorothy to her goal. When you look at your own charts assess whether the motivation will provide the push your character needs.

Every character is individual so it's difficult, if not impossible, to draw up a list of motivations and label them "weak."

But you can, within the context of your own story, assess whether your character's motivation will give him all the impetus he needs to take on his challenge.

Now for the flip side—internal motivation

Dorothy's chart is looking better, but we still have to deal with the internal GMC. Remember that the internal components of GMC are the emotional elements of your story. Therefore the internal motivation should create emotion in the character.

Why is Dorothy looking for her heart's desire? Why does she want to find a place with no trouble? That answer is also given to us during the black and white part of the film.

Dorothy is looking for her heart's desire because she's unhappy. This motivation resonates with truth. Every teenager I know is unhappy about something. Or everything. Dorothy is no exception.

Her internal goal and motivation are logical for a teenager. It makes perfect sense. We can understand Dorothy, because we've all been there ourselves. She's unhappy because she's had a really bad day. The Margaret Hamilton character is after her dog. Dorothy falls in a pig sty. No one has time for her or will talk to her. Auntie Em and her Uncle are mad at her. There's a tornado.

Using warped teenage logic, Dorothy figures that if she can find that place with no trouble, that place she really wants...if she can find her heart's desire, she'll be happy. This is an emotional element. This is not something you can touch or see or hear. This is the sort of character baggage that evolves into a life lesson. Clearly emotional, not physical.

Dorothy	EXTERNAL	INTERNAL
Goal	GET HOME 1 Get to Emerald City 2 See the Wizard 3 Get the broomstick	To find her heart's desire and a place with no trouble.
Motivation	AUNTIE EM IS SICK 1 The Wizard is there. 2 He has the power to send her home. 3 The price for sending her home.	1 She's unhappy. 2 Trouble follows her everywhere.
Conflict		

A match made in heaven

Keep in mind that your goals, motivations, and conflicts need to match your characters. A sixteen-year-old lead character is probably not going to be worrying about retirement. A sixty-year-old is not going to be worried about the prom.

Every character's GMC is different. Every writer's execution of GMC is going to be different. That's okay. It's your character and your book. No one should tell you what will work and what won't work. Which GMC is too light and which is too complicated.

Because every writer will develop GMC differently you'll have to experiment, but remember everything flows from your character. Make sure your characters are the sort of people who would actually make the necessary choices that propel your story forward.

Judge your GMC and your characters not by one isolated negative comment, but by honestly answering these questions:

> Is the goal important to the character?
> Is the motivation urgent?
> Is the goal within the realm of possibility?
> Does the character have skills and flaws that make this story unique to him?
> Can you use this GMC to help the reader understand your character?

If, however, you collect a bouquet of negative comments, you need to re-evaluate.

When someone tells you that your story is not believable, it isn't because you sent the characters to a space planet. It's not because your character cured cancer. It's because your GMC wasn't logical. Your GMC wasn't appropriate to your characters. What the reader is telling you is, "I didn't believe these people would find themselves in this situation or make these decisions."

At that point you have to either tinker with GMC or tinker with your characters. For example....

You're going to have to work pretty darned hard to sell the reader an insurance salesman doing emergency surgery in the jungle with a pair of barbecue tongs, a clothespin, and a Swiss Army knife.

A fireman is better. Now if that fireman is a paramedic, who walked away from an internship, then you have a character who's slipped quietly into the realm of possibility. Give him the downed plane's emergency kit, and you're well on your way to fixing the problem. You've fixed the character.

Or stick with the insurance salesman and up the ante. Motivate him. It's his little girl turning blue on the jungle ground. She's the one who can't breathe and needs an airway. Everyone else is dead, and she's choking. Now give the insurance guy the Swiss Army knife and a tube from a ball point pen. I think maybe he just might be motivated enough to try it. He doesn't have much choice, does he?

If there is compelling motivation, you can make us believe. Laying the foundation of motivation is like knitting. If you miss a stitch, you have to go back and pick it up. Sometimes all you need is an additional sentence or a little change in the character's background.

Coincidence cannot replace motivation.

Too often I read beginning writers whose characters feel more like dolls aimlessly pushed around by the author into circumstances designed to elicit the maximum amount of humor or danger. If the author wants tension and danger, he conveniently breaks the heroine's car, strands her in a strange town, sticks her in a bed-and-breakfast, and then sends the poor woman, in her nightgown and without a weapon, to investigate screams coming from a closed door at the end of a deserted hallway. To make matters worse, blood is pouring from beneath the door.

Instant tension and suspense. Right? Wrong!

The reader isn't on the edge of his seat. He's rolling his

eyes. "Aw, come on! How stupid can she be? Why isn't she running the other way? To a phone! To get a weapon!" You'd better have sufficient motivation to send her down that hallway or the reader simply won't stay with you. A string of coincidences culminating in character stupidity do not make a believable story.

Most individuals will not put their lives at risk without good reason. Personal safety instructors routinely instruct their students to yell, "Fire!" instead of "Help!" People will run to put out a fire, but they won't come help if you're in trouble. This is the sad state of human nature at the moment, and your reader is probably going to be a human. Therefore, he knows exactly what the average person is likely to do.

Investigating screams in your underwear, without a gun, falls squarely into the unlikely category.

Unless your character is spellbound by some supernatural force as in horror, science fiction, paranormal, or fantasy novels, this scene isn't going to work. Stupid characters without common sense do not make great heroes—no matter how much trouble they're in. And only a stupid character would go down that hallway.

What do you do?

Put the heroine's sister in that room, which gives the heroine a personal stake in the scream behind the door. Give her a gun and a background that insures we believe she'll charge into any situation to protect a human life. Or maybe her husband was killed because no one came to his aid when he was mugged, and she'll be damned if she'll stand there and let someone else die. There are a million ways to make the scene work.

The trick is motivation, not coincidence.

Wait a minute! The big writers use coincidence all the time!

Before everyone writes me letters, hold on. Yes, I know some wildly popular books were based on coincidence. John Grisham's *The Client* is one example. However, the coincidence is nothing without the decisions of the characters who were thrown into that accidental moment.

For those who don't know the opening of *The Client*, a Louisiana attorney (with dangerous mob secrets) chooses to commit suicide above the embankment where two boys are sneaking a smoke. Certainly a coincidence. Neither party planned for the arrival of the other. Neither party knew the other. But there they are. Coincidence. Fate. Whatever you want to call it.

However, everything that happens from that moment forward is driven by a specific character's reaction to the situation. Those of you familiar with Joseph Campbell's *Hero With A Thousand Faces* and Christopher Vogler's *The Writer's Journey* will recognize this scene as one of the defining moments of *The Client*. This accidental meeting is the "call to adventure" for Grisham's main character—an adolescent boy. When heroes are presented with a problem, challenge or an adventure, they are literally receiving a call to adventure—a call to take action. Heroes can refuse. Or they can accept.

In *The Client* the boy answers the call. He *chooses* to prevent the suicide. Assessing the risk as low, he chooses to crawl up to the car and pull out the garden hose, which is delivering deadly carbon monoxide from the exhaust pipe into the car window. The boy's choice has consequence.

Just as the character has a choice, so does the writer. You choose how you will open a story, how you will deliver the hero's call to adventure. Grisham could simply have had the boy wander into a public bathroom and see the attorney putting a gun to his head. Would that have been as effective? As strong? I don't think so. Because there would have been no conscious choice.

Character choices will always involve the reader more than simple coincidence.

Dorothy wasn't swept up in the tornado by accident. She was in the wrong place at the wrong time because of her own actions. She chose to run off into a storm because she was unhappy at home. She chose to run home in the storm because she was worried about her aunt. Dorothy had good reason for each of her actions.

In *The Client* the boy's action puts him squarely in the middle of a storm just as dangerous as the one Dorothy ventured into. Coincidence has faded. Replaced with choice, purpose, and action.

Examining different types of coincidence

Coincidence: *The failure of the author to properly lay a foundation and motivate the plot actions of his/her book.*

Ever read books or manuscripts and the scenes are... well...flat? Going nowhere? Read like filler? An example of this can best be illustrated as follows:

Question: "Why are your characters running into each other in the dry cleaners?"

Answer: "Well, I needed to get them together so the hero could say some sexual tension things about a fancy dress she's retrieving. It doesn't really belong to her but he doesn't know that."

Question: "Nothing else happens?"
Answer: "Well, no. Just sexual tension. They just run into each other. It's kind of a cute meet and they go from there."

The problem with this scene for a romantic comedy, as described, is that the only agenda in evidence is the *author's* agenda of a cute meet and sexual tension. The characters themselves have no sense of purpose. They're little more than paper dolls. Authors who just shove the characters around like race cars in a Monopoly game are asking for revisions and rejection.

If the characters run into each other at the dry cleaners, the hero had better be there as an officer of the court to shut down the business—put a lock on the door—because of a bankruptcy action, and the heroine had better be desperate to retrieve the designer evening gown she borrowed from her stuffy socialite sister without permission. With the scene constructed this way, the characters still end up in the same place at the same time and meet accidentally. But they each have a solid reason for being there.

In the new scene the heroine is motivated. She needs to convince the hero to let her inside, just for a minute. If she doesn't get that dress, she's going to have to confess to her sister—a fate worse than death—or sell her car to come up with enough money to replace the dress.

Even light comedy should be well motivated. It's foolish to assume that a shorter book needs any less attention in the GMC department. In fact, a shorter book needs stronger GMC. By that I mean clear, understandable GMC. Short books can't waste time rambling. You've got to set up your characters and get out of the way.

A writer can't afford five pages of backstory (character background) before getting to the point. Page space is too precious in books less than 65,000 words. External motivation is usually the most important to establish early in the book. Internal motivation can take a bit longer to develop and be woven into the fabric of the story one thread at a time.

Coincidence: *The failure of the author to properly develop backstory motivation for the characters.*

Here's another kind of coincidence you'll want to avoid. Don't you hate it when characters have no baggage? They step into the story as if they were sprung from a vacuum.

Consider a story in which the heroine and her adopted child move next door to the widowed hero and his adopted child. Surprise! Their children are obviously siblings or twins! Won't this be a fun story!

No.

No matter how fun the "Oops! Imagine that! We're related!" scene might be, it's not believable. And that's where coincidence kills a book. It jerks the reader out of the fantasy world long enough to roll his eyes and say, "Puh-lease! I don't believe this."

If you jar your reader, you might never get him back.

Certainly it's difficult to come up with a scenario in which there is no coincidence, in which the heroine chooses to find her child's sibling for a reason. It's harder still to come up with why she actually *moved* into the neighborhood instead of just knocking on the man's door or phoning him.

Remember, if it were easy, everyone would be writing.

But if you spend the time, if you dig deep enough into your characters and story, you can make this scenario work. And the book will be stronger. Hmm...what if the heroine's child isn't a twin or adopted at all? What if the heroine had to give up one of her children because she couldn't afford the baby's special medical needs? What if moving into the neighborhood is the only way she can watch her second child grow up? What if she broke the law to find out whom had adopted her child? If you play the "what if" game long enough, the coincidence will disappear. In it's place will be a backstory that motivates your heroine to move into the hero's neighborhood.

"What if" is also known as brainstorming.

The only good coincidence is the subconscious working.

The creative side of the brain is amazing. When you least expect it, you'll find yourself wondering how you could have been so brilliant.

Halfway through the book you remember a little throw-away line of dialogue, which the hero deadpanned as he got up on a kitchen step stool to retrieve a kitten from the top of the cabinet. He said, "I hate heights." You smiled and continued to write.

Now...halfway through the book, that little throw-away line is suddenly important. Your hero has unexpectedly been forced out onto a ledge. He says, "I hate heights." And you're feeling pretty darned clever. Suddenly that ledge looms large in the reader's mind, just as it looms large in the hero's mind.

That's a good coincidence, and it's the subconscious working. It's also a "call back." Good books draw on themselves and develop. They aren't a string of unrelated events, but rather the sum of character experience. Each scene changes the character and adds another dimension to his personality.

At least that's how it's supposed to work in a perfect world. Sometimes we aren't brilliant, and we don't think of the great kitchen line until the hero is out on the ledge. Don't worry. Revision is a wonderful thing. Just go back into the kitchen scene and add, "I hate heights."

More examples of motivation

You need to learn GMC by applying it to other people's work. Examine movies and books of different genres. No matter the subject matter, the basic question of motivation is still going to be "Why?"

> Why does Richard Kimball of *The Fugitive* want to find the man who killed his wife?
> *Because he wants to clear his name.*
> *Because he wants justice for his wife.*
> *Because he doesn't want to spend the rest of his life in jail.*

One of these motivations is urgent. All are compelling. Together these motivations are strong enough for us to believe each and every action Kimball takes in the movie. He is focused on one goal, pushed toward it by motivations that won't let him quit. This is of course external motivation. It relates to the concrete external goal of Kimball, which is to find the man who killed his wife.

This particular movie is tightly constructed. The internal motivation also feeds the external GMC. As I mentioned previously, we are left to piece together Kimball's internal GMC. Therefore, I'm listing a couple of motivations which suggest themselves in the movie. Neither is fully-developed, but they are strongly hinted.

> Why does he want to free himself from the guilt?
> *Because he is haunted by visions of his failure. He has nightmares and waking-mares that remind him of every detail of the killing.*
>
> *Because he'll never be able to go forward until he puts the past behind him.*

As in Dorothy's example, the internal motivation is something that creates emotion. Writers of romance novels should give the internal elements of GMC particular attention since romance novels are well-known for having an external story and an interior story. "Wounded heroes" can usually be understood by studying their internal GMC. In fact internal GMC is the best weapon a romance writer has for making the popular alpha male hero—the strong silent type—accessible to the reader. If you want the reader to fall in love with Rhett Butler, then the reader had better understand what makes the man tick. If we know what's important to him, we sympathize with him.

The Fugitive offers a good example of secondary character motivations. Deputy Marshal Gerard is like a dog with a bone.

> Why does he want to capture Richard Kimball?
> *Because he believes felons are dangerous.*
> *Because it is his duty to protect the citizens of the U.S.*
> *Because his reputation is on the line.*

Gerard's multiple external character motivations for this one goal are important. Through the course of the investigation Gerard will learn that Kimball is not dangerous. The man hasn't harmed a flea. Hasn't committed any crimes that injure people. He's even put himself at risk to save a young boy misdiagnosed in an emergency room. All his actions form the portrait of an innocent man trying to clear his name.

This felon isn't dangerous. Therefore one of Gerard's motivations is weakened. Fortunately, Gerard has two other motivations to draw on, two more that push him forward with the same determination as before. In fact, Kimball's escape during the jail scene is a personal prick to Gerard's ego. Gerard had Kimball in his sights, and Kimball still got away.

As one motivation weakens (Kimball is not dangerous) another motivation (Gerard's reputation) is strengthened. When using multiple motivations, be cognizant of the ways they can work to keep your character on task.

Motivating multiple goals

Casablanca's Rick Blaine has his hands full trying to balance his goals of keeping the bar open, punishing Ilsa, and getting Ilsa and Victor on a plane. At the beginning of the movie, the first two goals are of equal importance. By the end of the film, the goal of putting Ilsa on the plane is the most important goal.

> Why does Rick want to keep his bar from being closed down?
> *Because he wants to make money. The bar is his livelihood and the livelihood of employees who depend on him.*

Why does Rick want to punish Ilsa?
Because she left him in Paris.

Why does Rick want to get Ilsa on that plane?
Because it's the only way to insure her safety.

Ilsa's safety is an urgent matter. A matter requiring immediate attention if unpleasant consequences are to be avoided. Physical danger lurks behind every corner in *Casablanca*. Rick is very much aware of this fact.

At first glance the goals and motivations appear to be completely unrelated, and I've told you that multiple goals should crash into each other. So what gives? Keep in mind that the decisions Rick makes for goal number three (getting Ilsa out of Casablanca) could jeopardize his business. That fact ties these goals together. His awareness of the danger to Ilsa (which is the motivation for getting her on the plane) heightens his empathy and sense of responsibility to the other people who need him, making him more determined to keep his bar open. And we're right back to goal number one.

Each motivation impacts the other. Each goal impacts the other. Whether you paint the relationship between multiple goals with a broad stroke or with subtlety, the result is worth the effort. You'll have a more complex book and a more satisfying read.

Internally, Rick faces the same struggle for balance between his multiple goals. As with the external elements above, one of his internal goals eventually becomes more important, taking precedence over the other.

Why does Rick want to regain the love he lost in Paris?
Because the pain of Ilsa jilting him has never lessened.

Because in spite of his best efforts to forget her, he's still in love with Ilsa.

Why does Rick want to do what is right for the world?
Because he sees, first hand, what the war is doing to people.

Because he can't remain aloof any longer now that someone he deeply cares for is suffering because of the war.

Rick is a wonderfully complicated character, full of contradictions and self-made rules. Watching him rebuild his character, or perhaps rediscover his moral compass, is tremendously satisfying. Not only does Rick grow, Ilsa manages to do a bit of growing herself after struggling to achieve her goals.

Why does Ilsa want to get her husband out of Casablanca?
Because her husband is wanted by the Germans for subversive activities throughout Europe and for his escape from a concentration camp.

Because once her husband's safety is assured, she'll be free to stay with Rick, whom she still loves.

As you can see, Ilsa has one goal—to get her husband out. But she has a couple of motivations. Both valid. However, the second motivation listed deserves a closer look. That motivation will put her in conflict with Rick. She wants her husband gone so she can stay. Rick wants her to go to safety with her husband.

Looking at their external GMC side by side you can begin to see the conflict developing. Ilsa and Rick are, in a sense, both ally and enemy. This is an excellent combination for any relationship novel or buddy story.

Casablanca Comparison	**RICK EXTERNAL**	**ILSA EXTERNAL**
Goal	1 Keep bar open 2 Punish Ilsa 3 Get Ilsa and Victor on plane	Get husband on that plane
Motivation	1 Needs money and people depend on him 2 Because she hurt him when she left him in Paris 3 To insure her safety	1 He's in grave danger. 2 Once he's safe she can stay with Rick.
Conflict		

Ilsa—inside out

Her internal goal and motivation are a combination appropriate to a woman who's been through hell, as war and marriage to a hunted man must certainly be.

> Ilsa wants happiness with Rick and some personal peace. *Because she's tired of chasing around the world after her husband, constantly in danger, never knowing if he'll return from one of his meetings.*
>
> *Because she realizes she didn't marry Victor out of love. She married him out of respect, and respect is no longer enough.*
>
> *Because she can't lie to herself now that the difference between love and respect is right in front of her. She knows what she had with Rick in Paris was love.*

In comparison to her external GMC which is fairly straight forward, Ilsa's internal side is complicated and filled with strong emotion. She's a married woman in love with someone else. During the war, breaking marriage vows would not have been taken lightly. Ilsa's internal makeup gives the character, and the writer, an emotional mine field to explore.

Making a silk purse from a sow's ear

If you can tap into the reader's subconscious and make him

feel for the character, you can reform the unreformable. It's the motivation. A character can behave in a reprehensible way, in a way we would normally condemn, but if the motivation is strong enough, we'll forgive the character.

I once wrote a book in which the heroine is a hit woman. She kills people for money. She killed for the first time when she was twelve years old. Not a very heroic character to work with. The key to redemption was the motivation. (*Bad To The Bone*, Bantam Loveswept)

You can do anything—any character, any setting, any plot. You have complete freedom to create as long as you motivate.

Wrapping up

Motivation is your story's foundation. You can build your novel on quicksand or you can build on top of solid bedrock.

Important points to remember:

1. Motivation drives your characters.

2. First time authors should keep motivations simple, strong, and focused.

3. Strong motivation helps the reader suspend his disbelief and immerse himself in your story world.

4. Motivation is usually expressed in a sentence containing the word "because."

5. Urgency is as important for motivation as it is for goals.

6. All the character's actions and decisions should be motivated.

7. Motivation can never be too strong.

8. The GMC chart can help you visualize the relationship between your character's goal and motivation.

9. Goals and motivations should be appropriate to the character and his/her background.

10. Internal motivation should create emotion within the character or relate to a clearly emotional issue.

11. There is no "right" or "wrong" GMC as long as the author can sufficiently develop it.

12. Tinkering with the character's GMC components or tinkering with the character's background are both ways to get a book back on track.

13. Do not confuse coincidence with motivation.

14. Character choices involve the reader.

15. "Wounded heroes" can be understood by looking at their internal GMC. Emotional scars lend themselves beautifully to internal GMC.

16. Multiple motivations work to keep your character on task.

17. Characters can be both ally and enemy.

Chapter Four

CONFLICT: CAUTION! ROADBLOCK AHEAD!

Who. What. Why. Why not.

So far I've covered: who, what, and why. Character, goal, and motivation. That leaves us with "why not." Conflict is the "why not."

Conflict is the reason your character can't have what he wants. If your character *could* have what he wanted, then you have no book! Conflict is the obstacle or impediment your character *must* face in obtaining or achieving his goal. Conflict is not an optional element.

Conflict is ***required*** *in commercial fiction.*

Think of conflict as your ticket to the major leagues. If you can master conflict, readers will stampede the bookstore. You'll keep them up at night. And you'll impress the heck out of most editors.

Quick definitions of conflict

1. Conflict is a struggle against someone or something in which the outcome is in doubt.

2. Conflict is bad things happening to good people.

3. Conflict is bad things happening to bad people.

4. Conflict is friction, tension, opposition.

5. Conflict is two dogs and one bone.

Many are called. Few are chosen.

Let me warn you...if conflict makes you uncomfortable or you have difficulty wrecking the lives of your characters, you need to consider another line of work. In commercial fiction you need strife, tension, dissension, and opposition. If you omit these elements, you won't be able to sustain the reader's attention. Even in romance novels—known for their happy endings, sufficient conflict must exist to make the reader doubt the happily-ever-after.

Handy tip—
If the characters never face hardship...
If they're never in danger...
If they never struggle...
Your book is going to be boring.

On the other hand, if the thought of conflict and trouble makes you chortle gleefully and race to your computer, you are definitely in the right place. If you love conflict, chances are your characters will be flawed and in trouble. That's a good thing. Here's why:

> *People with perfect lives are boring, and...well...frankly, they're irritating.*

How many of you want to read a novel about a woman who wins a lottery, loses forty-seven pounds by cutting back on vegetables, is offered a starring role in a movie, marries her co-star Mel Gibson, wins an Oscar, and lives happily ever after? Not very many, I can assure you. Certainly none of the editors I've met over the years would be interested in this oh-so-charming plot. Even if an editor expressed an interest, once the publisher's marketing department got a look at the book, your print run would be about 175 copies.

Remember *The Perils of Pauline?* Nothing has changed since the movie serials. Today's reader still wants to see Pauline (or Paul) tied to the railroad tracks. We want to see the train coming. We want to feel slightly superior because we're not in that mess! And we don't have to find a way out of it. We like to see our characters tested. We want our characters to earn their rewards, just as we have to earn ours in real life.

Any writer interested in *publishing* commercial fiction has to get on the conflict bandwagon. Conflict equals disruption, and the reader wants to anticipate disruption. This is what keeps him turning the page. The reader is happiest when he can see the train coming, heading straight for poor Pauline.

Clearly defined conflict is a must.

Let me give you another warning about conflict. Get a grip on it. Know what the major impediment to your character's goal is and clearly define the conflict. Otherwise your reader may feel bombarded by conflict, unable to sort out the important issues from the peripheral issues. Unrelenting conflict or throwing "everything but the kitchen sink" at the character can numb the reader.

Imagine a historical romance in which the hero killed the heroine's father. The heroine owns land that the hero needs for his ranching operation. The heroine was once a prostitute, and the hero has no respect for prostitutes. The hero owns the bank that carries the note on the heroine's farm. The hero's younger brother is engaged to the heroine. The heroine is afraid of men because her father was abusive. The hero is secretly part Native American and knows that no respectable woman will have him. The heroine's dream is to open an orphanage for unwanted children, but the hero has sworn never to have children because he fears his own violent nature.

See? There is so much conflict between the hero and heroine, the reader may feel overwhelmed.

Another example of "everything but the kitchen sink" is the action film genre. The climax of thriller movies is extended. The viewer believes the hero has won, only to find victory snatched from his hands. Over and over again. Constructing a thriller forces the writer/filmmaker to walk a fine line. How much conflict is enough? How many times does the hero have to defeat the bad guys before he wins? We've all seen movies that we thought would never end. By the time the hero kills/arrests the bad guy, we don't care anymore.

Even lighter books such as romantic comedies need clearly

defined conflicts. Obviously you won't want to use heavy emotional conflicts in lighter books, but you can still create strong conflicts which will keep heroes and heroines apart emotionally. Consider lightening your romantic conflict by reducing the impact by one degree.

Heavy: Your heroine is afraid of large men with quick tempers because she was abused by her father and husband.

Lighter: Your heroine is afraid of large men with quick tempers because her sister was abused by her husband.

Heavy: Your hero was adopted and wants a large family but your heroine can't have children.

Lighter: Your hero was adopted and wants a large family but your heroine raised her five brothers and only wants her freedom from parenting now.

Another pitfall, which stems from fuzzy conflict, is erratic or slow pacing because you wander through scene after scene trying to get a handle on what the real battle is, what the character's real problem is. You'll miss the opportunity for foreshadowing and building to your book's climatic moment.

However, knowing your conflict allows you to focus, to toss out the scenes that don't work and do nothing to advance the plot. Knowing your conflict allows you to convey the character's emotions more clearly as the character experiences a setback or gains a small victory. Knowing your conflict allows you to create tense scenes because you know what's at stake for the character. You know exactly how the character feels, how he will react to each obstacle you put in his path.

When writing complex stories with multiple characters and multiple points of view, the same suggestion applies. Make sure that you know the individual GMC of each character. Make sure you have their conflicts planted firmly in your brain as you write. A success for one character may be a setback for another.

Make sure their GMCs collide. Eventually their paths or goals must intersect. Otherwise you are writing separate books in the same manuscript

We're off to see the Wizard. Again.

Dorothy's external conflict is an easy one—the Witch. She must fight the Witch during her entire journey to the Emerald City. She must fight the Witch to get the broomstick—the Wizard's price for sending her home. The Witch has no intention of giving up the broomstick. What's more, the Witch wants the ruby slippers Dorothy has on her feet.

In *The Wizard of Oz* Dorothy has a character—the Wicked Witch—standing squarely in her way as a conflict. The big overriding conflict for a book can be almost anything, but villains make excellent, well-defined conflicts. In *The Wizard of Oz* the Witch is the bad guy, the villain. The Witch is what Dorothy must overcome to get back home to Kansas.

Since the bad guy is a physical entity...one that impedes Dorothy's external goal, this makes the conflict external. The Witch is someone we can see, touch, and hear. We can smell her vile flying monkey familiars, and we can taste the brimstone in the air. All five senses are engaged. It's an easy call. The Wicked Witch is external—a classic example of external conflict.

Dorothy	EXTERNAL	INTERNAL
Goal	GET HOME 1 Get to Emerald City 2 See the Wizard 3 Get the broomstick	To find her heart's desire and a place with no trouble.
Motivation	AUNTIE EM IS SICK 1 The Wizard is there. 2 He has the power to send her home. 3 The price for sending her home.	1 She's unhappy. 2 Trouble follows her everywhere.
Conflict	1 THE WITCH 2 The balloon lifts off without her.	

Yes, you can have multiple conflicts, too.

You'll notice Dorothy's chart shows multiple conflicts. The Witch isn't her only problem. There is one last conflict, one last dying gasp of trouble for her to overcome. *But* the reader is treated to a single defined conflict through most of the movie. The last conflict—the balloon lifting off—is an important element. It's not a sub-conflict of the witch. It's not tacked on to the movie simply to increase the length or add another chill. It is a true conflict.

But for now, let's just focus on the Witch, who is Dorothy's major conflict. We'll get to the balloon eventually.

The purpose of conflict

In *The Wizard of Oz* two characters are pitted against one another in a battle of wills. Conflicts test your character. Characters who are tested usually experience character growth. Otherwise what's the point?

Dwight Swain, who wrote a number of incredibly informative writing texts, said that cowards make great heroes. Opposition enables a character to dig within himself, to rise to the challenge, to grow, and to become heroic. America loves an underdog.

Every person watching *Jurassic Park* was rooting for the humans, *not* for the dinosaurs. In the movie *Independence Day*, the aliens clearly have the upper hand. Yet, the characters continue to fight, becoming heroes in the process—even the drunken crop duster. In *The Hunt For Red October* the Alec Baldwin character must overcome his horrendous fear of flying in order to achieve his goal. He has to put himself in situations he's never faced before.

Cowards and courage make for great conflict.

Embodied within the statement above is the idea that imperfect heroes are the most satisfying because true courage is facing what you fear, trying even though the odds of failure are great.

Internal conflict made easy

Conflict is not limited to outside interference. Sometimes the strongest conflicts to achieving a goal are the character's own emotional roadblocks. Internal conflict is what keeps the character from learning his life lesson. Internal conflict is emotional conflict.

Goals, motivations, and conflicts come in all shapes and sizes. Just as in real life, your character may have one goal he admits to the world and one secret emotional goal known only to him. He may have one obvious motivation and one of which he is not yet aware. A character's journey can be of self-discovery. He may struggle against others and within himself.

Having inner and outer GMC makes your character multi-layered, which gives your book subtext and depth. Internal and external GMC give your scenes bite.

Dorothy spills her guts.

Finally, we've come to the end of Dorothy's chart. What's her internal conflict? What prevents her from learning her life lesson? What prevents her from finding her heart's desire?

She doesn't know what she wants.

How can she find a place with no trouble, a place where she'll be happy if she doesn't know what she wants and has no idea what will finally make her happy? She can't. Therefore, this indecision creates the conflict to achieving her goal.

Once again consider the appropriateness of Dorothy's GMC for a sixteen-year-old. Teenagers don't know from minute to minute what they want out of life. And once they decide, that's not really what they want anyway! They want something else entirely.

Take a look at Dorothy's completed chart. Pay particular attention to how the elements work together. (And no, I have not forgotten the balloon. I'm getting there. Don't rush me. You'll find out about the balloon in Chapter Six.)

Dorothy	EXTERNAL	INTERNAL
Goal	GET HOME 1 Get to Emerald City 2 See the Wizard 3 Get the broomstick	To find her heart's desire and a place with no trouble.
Motivation	AUNTIE EM IS SICK 1 The Wizard is there. 2 He has the power to send her home. 3 The price for sending her home.	1 She's unhappy. 2 Trouble follows her everywhere.
Conflict	1 THE WITCH 2 The balloon lifts off without her.	She doesn't know what she wants.

Wicked Witches, thieves, and other assorted villainous types

The strength of your book is your conflict. For many writers that sentence should read, "The strength of your book is your villain."

How many of us could forget the secondary villain of *Silence Of the Lambs?* Hannibal Lector is as evil as they come, but he looms large in our memory because he was a worthy opponent. He had an agenda that threatened to swallow up (literally) anyone who crossed his path. Our respect for the young female FBI agent grew as she forced herself to face her fears and crawl inside Hannibal's mind.

The Wicked Witch from Oz earned her place as a worthy opponent because she, too, had an agenda—her very own GMC. The internal side is only hinted at in the movie, so I've improvised a bit for the chart on the next page.

Wicked Witch	EXTERNAL	INTERNAL
Goal	The ruby slippers	Respect
Motivation	The slippers will make her the most powerful witch in Oz.	She's always felt inferior to her sister and the other witches.
Conflict	Dorothy won't give them up. (Glenda the Good Witch of the North told Dorothy not to take those shoes off her feet.)	Respect has to be earned. It can't be stolen.

The movie is powered by the Witch's GMC as much as by Dorothy's GMC. The conflict of the movie is the Witch's effort to get those slippers. The only way to get those slippers is to do something bad to Dorothy so she'll give them up or to kill Dorothy before she has a chance to get out of Oz altogether.

One last warning about conflict and how to nurture it

Conflict should not spring full-blown into your book like an unannounced house guest. The writer must lay a foundation for conflict, create believable goals, motivate the characters, and nurture the conflict to the inevitable crisis or climax. Otherwise your book becomes one long monotonous replay and rehashing.

Escalate the events in your book.

Move from the vague hint to the concrete. Introduce obstacles, each more difficult than the last. Introduce clues and uncertainties that spell disaster as they pile upon each other. When the climax of your book finally rolls around the reader will nod his head and say, "Yep. I could have told them two hundred pages ago, if they'd only asked me. I knew something bad was going to happen."

Readers like to see the train coming.

Certainly you don't want to write a predictable book. What I'm suggesting is that readers enjoy the anticipation. They enjoy guessing. Murder mystery fans are excellent examples of armchair plotters. Romance readers love the chase, the sexual tension. Fantasy readers enjoy guessing which rabbit the sorcerer is going to pull out of the hat next. The trick to keeping a reader on the edge of his seat is making sure he's bought into your story world. If he has, the reader is going to be worried about your character.

Remember? Conflict creates the worry. Knowing something bad will happen does not mean that the reader knows when or where or who or how or the ultimate outcome. But for heaven's sake give them that uneasiness in the pit of their stomachs. Raise the hair on the backs of their necks.

Step by step

If you rented *The Wizard of Oz* you were treated to an excellent example of how conflict is nurtured. Let's take a look at how conflicts with the Witch build and grow more frightening with each scene. Notice how the conflict grows from the vague to the concrete. From the verbal to the physical.

1. The Witch warns Dorothy in front of witnesses at the Munchkin Village. Could the movie maker have been any more direct in pointing out the problem Dorothy was about to face? No. The fact that the Witch is indiscrete in her warning tells us something about her desperation for those slippers. We know she's going to be trouble.

2. Next we see the Witch hiding behind the trees in the apple orchard. This is a very sneaky thing to do. This is our clue that this is an underhanded villain. There will be no face-to-face gunfight at high noon with an equal chance for all involved. Nope. This villain will use whatever devious trick is necessary to get those slippers.

3. Then she shoots fire at the scarecrow. Bingo! Concrete conflict. You can't get much more physical than this. Shooting fire at the scarecrow removes any doubt we have as to how far the Witch will go to obtain those slippers. Until this point we harbored suspicions. Now our suspicions turn to certainty. The Witch isn't devious; she's dangerous.

4. She drugs them in a poppy field. This scene shows us the power of the Witch is beyond the small displays we've seen so far. She can manipulate the environment. Pretty powerful stuff. Our estimation of the Witch goes up a notch; hope begins to fade.

Small red warning lights start to blink on our conflict sensors.

5. To make absolutely certain we understand the villain with whom we are dealing, the filmmaker shows us the Witch's creepy castle fortress and her vile flying monkeys. This is sort of a pop quiz for those who weren't paying attention earlier in the movie. Is the Wicked Witch really a villain? Yes. Just look at where she lives and with whom she associates.

6. When the Wizard asks for the Witch's broomstick as his price for sending Dorothy home, we all gasp. I've seen small children mouth the word "no" at the television screen. Because they know the task is impossible. They've seen the Witch in action. Dorothy's going to get herself killed. Heck, adults aren't too sure about this. We've seen her fortress and those nasty monkeys.

The payoff

This defining moment of conflict—the moment in which Dorothy must choose to face the Witch—is what the story has been working toward. This is one of the disasters we have been anticipating. This is the moment a less motivated character would walk away.

But Dorothy can't. She *must* get that broom. She *has* to get home. Auntie Em is sick and needs her.

GMC is a package deal. One element leads to and supports the next. The elements circle back on each other. A finely crafted

GMC is a work of art. Each piece—goal, motivation, and conflict—are necessary to the whole.

Build a foundation. Plant the seeds of worry in your reader's mind. Let them anticipate. And then deliver the conflict as promised. Some writers do this instinctively. Some writers plan carefully. Others go back and fix it later. No matter how you write, always deliver the conflict.

Some common beginner mistakes

Not every beginner makes conflict mistakes, but I have seen a pattern develop over the years of judging contests and reviewing the work of my university class.

Bickering is not conflict. Not only does bickering fail as true conflict, it's annoying to many readers. As with any "rule" there are exceptions. A few writers are known for their ability with witty repartee. However, there is a vast difference between witty repartee and bickering. *To bicker is to engage in a petty squabble.*

Take a look at your scenes and judge your characters' verbal disagreements against that definition. Are they arguing for argument's sake or is there a real problem at issue? A problem they will solve by discussion? Does the argument continue virtually unchanged from chapter to chapter, with the characters picking up where they left off? If you're writing romance, romantic suspense, or romantic comedy, be especially on guard against the temptation to substitute bickering for genuine conflict. It's all too easy for characters who "spar" to fall into the bad habit of bickering. Regardless of genre.

Another reason bickering doesn't qualify as true conflict is that it never progresses beyond words. Words are vague. You want to move your conflict from the vague to the concrete. You want to build an inevitable crisis. Bickering won't take you where you want to go.

If the villain of your thriller does nothing more than lob cheap shots at your protagonist, well, there's not much meat in the book.

Misunderstanding is never to be confused with conflict. If your characters in rocky relationships can sit down and resolve some misunderstanding, then you don't have conflict. If your hero can explain his fingerprints on the gun, you don't have conflict. If your heroine can explain to her boyfriend why she spent the night with a strange man, you don't have conflict. Most human beings are only too happy to offer excuses for their actions and to correct those around them.

Ask yourself if you are trying to build a book out of a misconception or misinterpretation of events. If so, ask yourself whether a reasonable adult would be able to communicate the truth. "Why no, Betty! I wasn't cheating on you! That was my sister sitting with me in the restaurant. Here's her picture in the old high school annual." When writing suspense, certainly don't wait until they put the hero in the electric chair before you have him finally confess his extramarital affair and alibi.

Misunderstanding could provide a brief minor conflict, but readers get restless when you try to extend a simple misunderstanding into the book's central conflict. Even as a minor conflict, misunderstanding should be weighed carefully and evaluated for its contribution to the story as a whole.

Now the disclaimer: Misunderstanding can work. It works best when used as the structure for a comedy of errors. In that type of comedy, the reader is *expecting* a chain of events to create chaos.

The conflict grows as one misunderstanding after another is piled on top of the first one. The first harmless lie leads to a second and then a third.

Before you know it the character needs a ladder to climb out of the hole. Notice that the misunderstandings are multiple. The consequences grow increasingly severe.

For the reader the anticipation comes from trying to guess when the house of cards will fall. They wonder what will trip up your character. Mine fields are everywhere. What will happen when the truth comes out?

Regardless of whether you are writing comedy or a thriller, the only justification you have for allowing a misunderstanding to blossom is motivation. You can do anything you want in fiction as long as you motivate the characters. If you have strong, urgent reasons for allowing a misunderstanding to go uncorrected, then you can make your plot work.

Examples of conflict

When we last left Luke Skywalker, he was off on a mission to rescue the princess, help the rebels, and to learn the ways of the force. What stands in his way? Darth Vader. But Darth Vader is more than a singular villain. He also represents the power of the Empire, the force of the fleet. He is a fully trained Jedi Knight—even though he has "gone over" to the dark force. Darth Vader is everything Luke is not: powerful and experienced.

This contrast with Luke makes Darth Vader a strong opponent, who affects Luke in a personal way.

Smaller conflicts for Luke:

1. He has no transportation off his planet.

2. The Empire is combing the universe for his droids.
3. The Princess' precise location on the Death Star is unknown.
4. Luke's backup (Han Solo) can't be trusted.
5. Obi Wan is killed before Luke can be trained.

Princess Leia has her own GMC. She wants to get the Death Star plans to the rebel camp and save them because her loved ones and friends are there. She wants to bring down the evil Empire because of their oppression. Those are her goals and motivations. What's stopping her from reaching her goals?

Darth Vader also functions as her large conflict. She's a prisoner. Vader knows the secret location of the rebel base. He has the power to destroy the entire planet on which the rebel base is located.

Sharing a conflict bonds Luke and Leia, making them allies. They also share a goal as Luke throws in his lot with Leia after saving her, vowing to help the rebel cause. Han Solo doesn't quite qualify as ally. He's more of a hired gun. He's in this mess for the money because he's got to pay off some debts before his creditors kill him. His conflict is the mission. If anything goes wrong (which it does!), if the princess ends up dead, if he can't get them off the Death Star, if he can't outrun the Imperial star cruisers...then he can kiss his money good-bye.

Star Wars is an example of multiple heroic characters with individual GMCs. This is clearly Luke's story, but the other characters each have fully developed GMC. Both of the male leads grow and change during the course of the movie.

The Fugitive also offers multiple characters for study. The reason Kimball can't find the man who killed his wife is that he's a known felon, a wanted fugitive and can't move freely in search of evidence. Deputy Gerard can't catch Kimball because Kimball has a head start. Gerard is starting from behind and Kimball is a clever adversary. He's not the ordinary fugitive hunted by Gerard. This point is subtly made in the movie when the marshals quickly track down and apprehend the other escapees.

For Ilsa Lund-Laslow in *Casablanca* the conflict to getting her husband out is their lack of visas. The French prefect refuses to issue them visas. The man, who was to procure stolen exit visas, is killed. Without a visa, they can't leave.

Ilsa and Victor want to leave Casablanca because Victor is pursued for his subversive activities, but they can't get visas.

Just as the word "because" triggers a clause of motivation, the word "but" triggers a clause of conflict.

Examples of internal conflict

Rick Blaine wants to recover the love he had in Paris, but he can't because the woman he loves is married. Off limits. He also wants to do what's right for the world, which means sending Ilsa away to support her heroic important husband, but she begs to stay—weakening Rick's resolve.

Internal conflict usually adds subtext and extra meaning to the external conflict. *Casablanca* can be used as an example of how the internal GMC adds meaning to the external. One of Rick's external goals is to get Ilsa on the plane. That particular goal is undermined because he must balance her *physical* safety against his happiness. And against her happiness.

Physical versus emotional. Rick is at war with himself. He is struggling against others and against his own emotions.

Two dogs, one bone—an example of external and internal conflict

This example was inspired by the old one line definition of conflict that is generally credited to Dwight Swain—two dogs, one bone. Patricia Keelyn, a published writing pal, and I decided to put this theory to the test in a workshop we once did on conflict. Could we actually create an internal and external conflict from two dogs and one bone?

OUR CAST OF CHARACTERS:

> *Fido*— an overgrown German shepherd who hasn't had anything to eat for two days. He's dirty, scruffy and looks like he's lost as many dog fights as he's won. He's reduced to scavenging for food wherever he can find it.
>
> *Fifi*— a French poodle and former beauty queen fallen on hard times after being dumped by the dog of her dreams. Her once perfectly-groomed white fur is now dirty brown and overgrown. All her carefully manicured claws are ragged and broken. She has a look of desperation about her, and is also out scavenging for food.
>
> *The Puppies*— six of them—off to the side—each looking like a strange combination of French poodle and great dane. They're all starving.

Into the midst of Fifi and Fido, we drop a bone. Both of them want the bone. Both are starving. Both make a play for the precious morsel of food. Fifi has never had to fight for anything in her life, and although she's well motivated, she's outclassed. Fido snatches the bone and turns to leave with his prize, but as he does, six hungry puppies begin to cry pitifully.

Oh, no! his conscience screams. *Only an insensitive rottweiler jerk would take food from hungry puppies! And your sainted mother didn't raise you to be a rottweiler.*

You have just witnessed both external and internal conflict.

Both Fifi and Fido wanted the bone for survival. They struggled against each other. That's external. It was a physical fight, which Fido won. However Fido hesitates once he has won the bone from the fair Fifi. Now he must struggle against his own moral code for the bone. That's internal.

Conflicts produce a winner and a loser. *Unless* the combatants find a way to compromise. Romance novels in particular require compromise. Otherwise there can be no happily-ever-after.

Compromise comes from within. Hence the importance of the internal GMC.

For those of you wondering...yes, Fido does give up the bone.

Wrapping up

Readers want characters to earn their rewards. Solid, well-constructed conflict insures the reward won't be too easy to obtain.

1. Conflict is the obstacle or impediment your character *must* face in obtaining or achieving his goal.

2. Know what the major impediment to your character's goal is and clearly define the conflict.

3. Unrelenting conflict or throwing "everything but the kitchen sink" at the character can numb the reader.

4. Make sure the GMCs of multiple characters collide. The collision creates conflict.

5. The central conflict for a book can be almost anything, but villains make excellent, well-defined conflicts.

6. Characters may have multiple conflicts just as they have multiple goals and motivations.

7. Conflicts test your character. Characters who are tested usually experience character growth.

8. Internal conflict is emotional conflict.

9. Having internal and external GMC makes your character multi-layered, which gives your book subtext and depth.

10. The strength of your book is your conflict.

11. The writer must lay a foundation for conflict, create believable goals, motivate the characters, and nurture the conflict to the inevitable crisis or climax.

12. Bickering is not conflict.

13. Misunderstanding is not conflict.

14. The word "but" in a GMC sentence precedes the clause dealing with conflict. Dorothy wants to get home to Kansas because her Auntie Em is sick *but* she must fight a witch on her way to the Emerald City to see the Wizard, who has the power to send her home.

15. Internal conflict usually adds subtext and extra meaning to the external conflict.

16. Conflicts produce a winner and a loser. Unless there is compromise.

Chapter Five

CONFLICT MASCOTS

(and other ways to heighten conflict)

Conflict dies without a mascot or a focal character.

Patricia Keelyn and I often discuss the craft of writing. Particularly when we're scheduled to give a joint workshop at a conference. One such workshop was on conflict. Since "interactive" is the buzz word of the nation, we thought the workshop should be interactive as well.

Our first gambit to involve the audience in an experience of conflict was to pull five people from the audience to catch a bouquet. Now Patricia and I are both experienced writers, and we know how important motivation can be. We promised a crisp ten dollar bill to the person who caught the bouquet! (This also insured that we actually got volunteers instead of having to beg.)

We tossed the bouquet. One of the writers clawed her way through the pack and caught it.

POOF!

Instant conflict.

It's a piece of cake, right? All you need to do to create effective conflict is concoct a situation where two or more people struggle against each other. That's what I've just spent twenty pages telling you, right? That's what all the people in the workshop thought.

Wrong.

Okay, you're half right.

This *is* conflict, and certainly a step in the right direction. All five people wanted the ten dollars, and only one could have it, but this conflict was created by external forces only. These people stepped out of a vacuum and onto our stage. We knew nothing about them.

No one watching in the audience cared "who" caught the bouquet. Why didn't anyone care? Because the audience didn't know the participants—the bouquet catchers. And although ten dollars was at stake, we have to question whether the participants even cared that much.

Conflict requires a mascot. Conflict is all about character. Emotions are important. Motivation is critical. All the conflict in the world will not matter if the characters do not care deeply about the outcome. If your characters don't care, neither will your reader.

Character history makes a difference.

Now, I'll tell you something that made me care who won the ten dollars that day. After the workshop, a woman came up to get my autograph on a plain canvas book bag, which the conference was selling at its bookfair. As I scribbled my name, she told me how grateful she was for the ten dollars. That it had been a real struggle to find the money for this conference, and she was on a very tight budget. Even tighter since, right before our workshop, she had spent her dinner money on the canvas bag.

The bag was a gift for a terminally ill friend back home. She planned to have it autographed by all the published authors she could find as a way to brighten her friend's spirits. I don't know about you, but I suddenly cared very much who won that ten dollars. And if I'd known her backstory at the time we threw the bouquet, I would have been rooting for her.

The reader absolutely must have a guide through the maze of conflict.

So we're right back where we started—with character, the who of "who, what, why, and why not." Viewpoint is critical to making the reader feel as if he is experiencing the trouble right along with your character. Point of view cannot hover above the scenes. Get down in there! Ever heard the old expression that you don't know someone until you walk a mile in their shoes? Walk with your characters. Master point of view.

Give your reader a character he can care about and the conflict will double in intensity. You can even boost the conflict simply by carefully designing the circumstances of an event.

To illustrate this, let's create a scene. Our heroine has to go to school to pick up her niece. That's the scene, the event. Now, look at the two scenarios below.

> The niece is a perfect student.
>
> OR
>
> The niece is in the principal's office because she blew up the science lab.

The event is the same—a trip to school—but which scenario

is more interesting? Which story would make you turn the page to find out what happens? Which scenario makes you care about or empathize with the heroine?

Of course, you're more interested in the second scenario in which the niece has blown up the lab. Picking up an errant child from school and facing the principal is a universal experience. Every parent can empathize. If the reader doesn't have children, chances are still good that he is familiar with the circumstance from having been the offending school child. The reader can easily put him/herself in this situation and anticipate what will happen.

Raising the stakes

Consider the same event—the heroine must pick up her niece, who has blown up the school lab. But let's add a little meat to the bones of our character. In other words, let's give the character a little backstory. As with the woman who caught the bouquet, the history of a character can make all the difference in the strength of your conflict.

Our heroine blew up the exact same lab when she attended the school. The principal is the same principal she faced ten years ago.

This scene is now filled with tension because we have a mascot to guide us through the event. We are immersed in the scene from the point of view of the heroine. Poor woman!

Careful construction of your characters is one of the best techniques for heightening the impact of conflict.

What other techniques can you use to heighten conflict?

SETTING

If you're writing a dark suspense, set your book against a dark brooding setting such as the Northwest where it rains all the time. Or maybe New Orleans which is an intense locale which contributes swamps, graveyards, old southern homes filled with secrets. You can certainly write a suspense set at Disney World, but beautiful resort locales don't make the reader straighten their spine or look over their shoulder. You have to work harder to create a mood of tension if you use a setting that is at odds with the tone of your book.

Imagine how difficult it would be to write a romantic comedy set in Ethiopia. Regardless of whether your romance is a contemporary or historical, setting is important. Historical romances derive conflict from the mores of the day. A heroine of the prairie would not have the same conflicts as a heroine of Regency England. Or a heroine of the Scottish Highlands.

Settings for science fiction and fantasy seem to be "easier" at first glance because the writer creates his world. However the same challenges face the fantasy and science fiction writer. He must still match setting to the tone of his book. Or play against the contrast of the setting.

Whether you match or contrast your setting with the tone of your book, be aware that this element affects your conflict.

FISH OUT OF WATER

Toss your character in a strange environment. Consider poor old Indiana Jones, the quiet college archaeology professor. He's taken away from his college, the museum, teaching, and his dull predictable life; he's thrown into adventures in foreign countries. He's forced to live by his wits because he's a fish out of water. The familiar can no longer sustain him.

The conflict in a "fish out of water" story is immediately heightened because readers understand the tension of being thrown into a strange situation. They know how it feels to be without a social or cultural compass and without resources. Or they can imagine how it feels.

FORESHADOWING

This is something we all learned in high school English and promptly forgot. Dig this tool out of the closet and dust it off. Foreshadowing is used effectively in *Raiders of the Lost Ark*, the first Indiana Jones movie.

Indy is in the South American jungle at an ancient tomb. A rival archaeologist has just stolen his artifact. Indians are chasing him. The bad guy is shooting at him. He's dodging arrows. Finally he makes it back to the spot where his pilot is waiting, and he dives into the plane. Safe at last. Never once has he shown fear or indecision. He's been a strong, action-packed hero! Indiana Jones is a *real* man. Until he sees the snake in his cockpit.

Our brave Indy is completely undone, showing fear for the first time. "Oh, God. I hate snakes." The pilot is completely unsympathetic, casting Indy in the role of a wimp.

On the surface this sequence is just a gag, a moment of levity to break the tension of the chase. However, later in the movie Indy must go into an Egyptian tomb to recover the ark. They move the great stone slab and shine a light into the black pit. There are snakes in the pit. Millions of snakes.

The conflict and tension is immediately heightened because we know that Indy hates snakes. His reaction was foreshadowed by the scene in the plane. Now we wonder if he will actually go down into the tomb. We understand his conflict.

Simple Grammar and Writing Technique

Even the strongest conflicts will fall apart if you don't know how to convey the information to your readers. Words are your tools. You must know how to construct a sentence to enhance your pacing. You must know the type of story you are writing and what techniques work best.

Moments of strong conflict/tension in suspense usually require short sentences that convey action and imagery as quickly as possible. Imagine the final dramatic scenes of action adventure movies. Those scenes move! No close-ups of daffodils and cute puppies. You want to speed the pacing and send the reader hurtling toward the conclusion.

Study your genre, learn how writers use the techniques of style and grammar to deliver the conflict more effectively.

Point of View (or Viewpoint)

One of the easiest ways to heighten the impact of your conflict and create tension is to use point of view. If you have multiple characters in a scene and a choice of which character's POV to be in, choose the character who has the most at stake—the most to lose or the most to gain. If a bank teller is being robbed, we don't want to be in the point of view of the gardener outside. We want to be in the POV of the teller or the robber or the off-duty cop who's next in line and who left home without his gun—a cardinal sin for a police officer. What's he going to do?

Uncertainty of the Outcome

You can increase conflict and tension by balancing the forces of good and evil in your book. Give your hero a worthy opponent, but don't make the villain so evil, so powerful it becomes impossible for your hero to win. Don't make your villain so weak and stupid that he's easily overcome.

You may need a collective protagonist to defeat your villain.

Many fantasy novels use this device when the evil sorcerer or witch is simply too strong for one individual. A group of characters band together, pooling their resources and information. In *The Wizard of Oz* Dorothy needs all the help she can get. The Scarecrow, Tinman, and Cowardly Lion provide the help.

Wrapping up

Conflict is like a garden that needs constant attention. In your writer's bag of tricks you have the tools to provide that attention. The techniques mentioned here are only a few examples of the tools available.

Your strongest tool for heightening conflict is a meaty character to serve as the focal point. Readers want to experience the story through a character with whom they can identify. So put a well-developed character with a history into the eye of your "conflict storm."

Chapter Six

A CLOSER LOOK AT THE GMC CHART

Every time I start a book, I use a GMC chart. I fill it in with incomplete sentences—just notes to myself of the issues involved. You don't have to write long flowing sentences. To begin a chart, it's enough to scribble:

GOAL	GET HOME
MOTIVATION	AUNT IS SICK
CONFLICT	WITCH

You don't have to waste time making fancy boxes and headings. You can write the external if that's all you have and add the internal later. But the act of writing character GMC information down on one piece of paper will remind you *what* you are pointing your people *toward*. From these simple notes you can develop your idea more thoroughly. You can add meat to this skeleton.

Experiment with your GMC charts. Don't feel tied to this

particular format. Over the years I've added a couple of extra items myself.

Tag lines

In the charts you've seen thus far in this book, I've left off what I call the "tag line." I place it across the top of the chart, and the tag line represents what the character learns.

To see the tag line "in action" let's use Dorothy, since we've already explored her GMC. What does she learn? She actually learns two things, and I imagine you already know what those lessons are.

There's no place like home. If you want to find your heart's desire, you must look within yourself.

Dorothy	EXTERNAL	INTERNAL
Goal		
Motivation		
Conflict		

The reason we understand Dorothy's tag line so well is the fact the filmmaker put those words into her mouth. She had the revelation and shared it with us. The scriptwriters made sure we understood what the movie was about by nurturing all the elements and then tied it up neatly. We felt good. We could leave Dorothy because we knew she'd learned her lesson.

Your characters have to learn their lessons, too. As a reader, I need to know that the story people I cared about are stronger now. I need to know that they haven't struggled in vain. Characters who change earn our respect.

In *Casablanca* Rick learns that one person can make a difference in the world. Ilsa learns to put the problems of the world before her own happiness. Ilsa's lesson is one that Rick shares. We respect them for their sacrifice.

Dominant Impression

This is a trick I picked up from Dwight Swain. The man is a master at explaining the craft of writing. If you don't already own his books, may I suggest you run out immediately and buy yourself a copy of *Techniques of the Selling Writer*? The idea of a dominant character impression is only one of the hundreds of helpful ideas you'll find in Swain's work.

When asked to describe an individual, the first image that comes to mind is the person's dominant impression. This is a handle we use to catalogue the people we know. Swain advocates the use of an adjective and a noun of vocation. I broaden that advice and simply use an adjective and a descriptive noun. I like the freedom to define my character's essence beyond a simple job title. So I use any noun that fits my impression of the character.

obnoxious ambulance-chaser
aggressive nurse
charming nuisance

More specifically—
Han Solo is a cocky smuggler.
Princess Leia is a royal rebel.
Richard Kimball is an innocent fugitive.
Deputy U.S. Marshal Gerard is a tenacious hunter.

Notice that a dominant impression isn't a physical description. Dominant impressions tell us something about the character of the individual. The impression gives us clues as to how the character will react in certain situations. For instance—an aggressive nurse and a soft-hearted caretaker will have completely different reactions when confronted with a stray dog wandering the halls of the hospital. One would call the dog pound. The other would take him home.

Choose your character's adjective and descriptive nouns carefully. You get bonus points for being specific. Notice the progression from a generic image to a unique and specific one.

a self-confident man
a self-confident outlaw
a cocky outlaw
a cocky smuggler

This impression hints at the character's flaws and skills. Imagine the skills and contacts a smuggler has. His methods are stealth and deception. The final picture of a cocky smuggler is specific and filled with possibilities.

When contest judges, critique groups, or editors tell you that your characters are behaving "out of character," go back to your dominant impression. Check your characters' responses. Are they consistent with the dominant impression you are trying to convey? Are your descriptions of your character consistent with the dominant impression? Why is your obnoxious ambulance chaser suddenly reticent?

Using dominant impressions you can get to the heart of "out of character" problems. You can even change dominant impressions of characters. The key is showing the reader how the character changes. Show the reader scenes which force or motivate the character to change.

I incorporate the dominant impression with the character's name and place it in the name box of the chart. You can place the adjective and noun wherever you would like. Below you'll see a blank chart with both tag line and dominant impression.

There's no place like home. If you want to find your heart's desire, you must look within yourself.

Dorothy unhappy teenager	EXTERNAL	INTERNAL
Goal		
Motivation		
Conflict		

GMC is really a map.

Think of the outer/external GMC as a road map. Think of the external squares as a way to get your book from point A to point B. It's a plot outline. These are the events that will key what happens in the book.

Think of the inner/internal GMC as a contour map. These squares will provide the emotional highs and lows of your book. These will help you establish what your character must learn.

When you have both inner and outer GMC working together, you have a "mature" book. You'll have depth not only in your story but in your characters. You'll even have depth in your theme.

Wrapping up

Tag lines and dominant impressions can be used to add value to your GMC charts. When thinking of the chart, think of it as a road map (for plot) and a contour map (emotional highs and lows).

Chapter Seven

BIG BLACK MOMENTS NEED GMC

The climax of a book is frequently referred to as a "big black moment" or crisis. The moment at which the character realizes all may be lost. The final moment which determines whether or not your character will achieve his goal. Remember that goals may change during the course of a book. The big black moment addresses the most current and urgent goal.

How your character resolves the conflict should have the biggest emotional impact (on your reader) of anything in your book. The resolution is the big payoff for which your readers have been waiting. Don't cheat them. Make 'em laugh. Make 'em gasp. Make 'em cry. Make it big. Make it count.

Make it emotional.

Require the character to grow or sacrifice. To take a risk. In a romance novel in particular, the conflict resolution must be a clear emotion-based choice.

GMC is a powerful tool for shaping the ultimate conflict in your book. For any scene to have impact on a reader, that reader must know what's at stake. From page one, if you are cognizant of your character's GMC, if you spend time developing motivation and increasing the urgency of your character's goal...you can't miss. The reader will know exactly what is at stake.

GMC is a road map. It points you and your reader in the right direction.

The outer conflict usually reveals or causes the big black moment, but it is the character's internal GMC which will resolve the big black moment. (Read that sentence one more time.) This is commonly referred to as character growth. When your character makes the final leap, when he learns his lesson, he has the strength to go beyond himself. The coward gains courage. Rick Blaine of *Casablanca* can let go finally of his bitterness and in doing so can let go of Ilsa. He can send her to safety.

Let's recap. You reveal the outer conflict. Let the character grow and become strong enough to deal with this final blow. Then she can resolve her problem or get herself out of danger.

Dorothy's darkest moment

Let's take a look at the big black moment in *The Wizard of Oz*. Some of you may think the Witch's castle was Dorothy's darkest moment. Dorothy was certainly at a low point, certainly outnumbered. But the true big black moment for Dorothy, the final conflict to her goal of returning home, is the moment the balloon lifts off without her.

The Wizard has already told her that there is no magic to send her home. The balloon is her only hope. When the balloon begins to rise, so does our fear. We know what's at stake.

The moment is so black for Dorothy because as soon as the balloon lifts off, she suddenly knows what she wants. Remember

Dorothy's internal conflict? She doesn't know what she wants. She's never going to find her heart's desire or a place where she's happy because she doesn't know what she wants.

As soon as the balloon is gone... ***Bam!*** Instantly she knows what she wants. It's home and family, and she's had it all along, but she threw it away. This is why the moment is so hopeless for Dorothy. She will never be able to get back home. Never be able to tell her aunt and uncle that she loves them.

All of this works so beautifully because the filmmaker gave us a nice big GMC handle. We understood the character.

The resolution

The Wizard of Oz is a fantasy. The resolution by necessity of remaining true to the genre has fantasy elements. However, the resolution itself is fueled by Dorothy's internal GMC.

The realization that home is her heart's desire allows Dorothy to use the power of the ruby slippers. In Oz you have to know what you truly want before the ruby slippers will do you any good. You have to be sincere. You have to believe in it and want it badly enough to trust the magic.

Glenda the Good Witch forces Dorothy to voice her character growth. The viewer of *The Wizard of Oz* isn't cheated. We are shown Dorothy's character growth. "There's no place like home. There's no place like home." Then she can click her heels and go home.

But I'm not writing fantasy.

Obviously if you are not writing science fiction or fantasy

you will not have a pair of ruby slippers handy. However, the principle still applies. Reveal the crisis. Make the character choose. Dorothy's indecision about her heart's desire evaporated. She made a choice.

In discussing big black moments and resolutions it is easier to deal with my own work. So, I'm going to use a romantic suspense—*Bad To The Bone*, because I know intimately how the GMC of the heroine contributes to the climax.

The heroine, a retired hit woman, must come out of retirement to protect a child and her own secret past. The man who brokered her contracts has been kidnapped. Internally, the heroine wants a chance to go back and change the past. She also wants to feel worthy of love.

She carries a tremendous burden of guilt, but not the guilt you might think. Although she killed for the government—only the slime of the world, no women, no children—her professional guilt pales in comparison to her personal guilt. As a child, the heroine survived a harrowing ordeal that her twin sister did not. Survivor's guilt has eaten away at the heroine for years. The heroine was always the bad twin, always the troublemaker.

The internal conflict is that no one can relive the past. She's doomed to replay the past in her memory forever, but she can't change it.

The big black moment occurs when the heroine has almost accomplished her goal of retrieving the kidnapped man and protecting the child. However, in a split second, the victory is snatched from her as one of the downed kidnappers raises a gun and fires toward the heroine and the adolescent girl. Someone is going to die.

The heroine must choose. She shields the child and takes the bullet. She can't reshape the past, but the heroine can change the future. In fact, in her mind, she *was* changing the past. This time the bad twin died.

There! I've condensed a 63,000 word book into a few short paragraphs. Or at least I've condensed the book concept and internal GMC of *one* character. Keep in mind that although this is a very strong romance, this is a *character* big black moment.

In a romance novel, you will also be required to deal with the romantic big black moment. The two crucial moments can occur simultaneously or separately, with the romantic black moment coming first. And neither crisis can be resolved until character growth has been accomplished.

In *Bad To The Bone* this heroine would not have dusted the kidnappers, saved the day, and ridden off into the sunset with the hero. She didn't feel worthy of love. This particular heroine had to die and be reborn. Obviously the hero's moment of character growth comes as the heroine takes the bullet. But that's another set of GMC concerns.

Each character in your book is on his or her own journey, dealing with external plot concerns and emotional issues. If you write multiple viewpoints then you owe the reader satisfaction. All the characters should grow and change during the course of your book.

The return of Fifi and Fido

Even dogs deserve a chance to grow. Here's another short demonstration of how an external element creates a black moment. If you'll remember, Fifi and Fido struggled against each other for a bone. Fido walked away a winner but relented and offered the bone to the puppies.

This is a simple telling of the story. Look for goal, motivation, and conflict as you read.

Fifi, an unwed mother of six puppies, is recovering from an abusive relationship and wants to find a way to support her brood. A dastardly Great Dane deserted her when he found out she was pregnant, and now she will never trust another male dog again, especially dark brooding types. But her "nurture" instinct is working overtime at the moment because of her status as a new mother, and her resolve weakens because Fido is in bad shape and has given up the bone for the sake of her puppies. Fifi offers to let him stay at her makeshift home in the old Walden barn.

She even offers to share the bone he has just given to her. Besides, she tells herself, he looks tough enough to scare off the coyote that keeps coming around at night. Fifi may have been pampered, but she's no fool. She can use all the help she can get.

Fido—the dark, wounded "loner" hero—has lost everyone he ever loved. He knows better than anyone that it's a dog-eat-dog world out there. He's been on the run from the dog catcher since he escaped from the evil puppy mill prison that forced him to father hundreds of puppies. Child support alone was killing him.

He can't afford to take on another family. Not emotionally or financially. He is finally free to make his own life, but he needs a safe place to hide.

As the days pass Fido, who has sworn to himself that he won't get involved again, that he won't care about anyone but himself...well...Fido finds himself falling in love. Becoming attached to the little puppies. He makes a deal with himself that he won't stay, but he *will* get the family back on its feet before he leaves. He hunts that day, hunts until he can barely walk. He brings back enough food to take care of Fifi and company for some time. He's ready to leave.

Night comes.

He's stealing away when all hell breaks loose. The coyote attacks and Farmer Walden discovers the puppies at the same time. Fido has a choice. He can leave. Or he can protect the family he's come to love.

Uh oh! Protecting them means facing prison again. Farmer Walden will sell him back to the puppy mill or take him to doggie jail—the dog pound. Fido has dreamed of freedom all his life.

Will Fido risk his freedom to save Fifi and the puppies?

Of course. What's freedom if not the chance to participate in the world? To make a difference? To protect the ones you love? To be a part of something instead of isolated? In the process he saves Farmer Walden's life and they all live happily ever after on the farm.

This black moment is brought about by the external event. But it is the internal choice, the compromise, the character growth that keys the resolution.

Wrapping up

Big black moments are critical to the reader's final opinion of your book. Was it worth their time? Or did the book fizzle out? Use GMC to add depth to your character's crisis.

1. The climax of a book is frequently referred to as a "big black moment" or crisis.

2. How your character resolves the conflict should have the biggest emotional impact (on your reader) of anything in your book.

3. Require the character to grow or sacrifice.

4. The outer conflict usually reveals or causes the big black moment, but it is the character's internal GMC which will resolve the big black moment.

5. Reveal the crisis. Make the character choose.

6. Character black moments and romantic black moments *both* exist in romance novels. They may occur simultaneously or separately. The character growth must be achieved before either moment can be resolved.

7. Each character in your book is on his or her own journey, dealing with external plot concerns and emotional issues.

Chapter Eight

DON'T LISTEN TO YOUR MOTHER. GO AHEAD. MAKE A SCENE.

Once you have organized your thoughts into a coherent GMC chart, it's time to ask yourself if your GMC is going to lend itself to scenes. Can you work with it? Is it going to provide a beginning, a middle, and an end for your book? Can you show character growth? The book's turning point? Don't *tell* us about character growth or crisis. You've got to show it. How about conflict? Can you develop the conflict with the characters and the GMC that you've created?

The answers to all those questions are found in "scenes." Even if you've already finished a draft of the manuscript, ask yourself these questions about scenes already written.

Why?

Commercial fiction relies heavily on scenes. Readers want you to pick up the pace, cut to the chase, and zero in on the action. Readers want characters who *do* something. In other words, the scene is a fiction writer's best friend.

Very few books are written *entirely* in scenes. Most writers have a blend of narrative, internal monologue, description, etc. That distinctive blending of the elements of fiction creates a writer's voice and style. Regardless of style, you will use scenes. So learn to use them effectively. Make sure they showcase your character's GMC.

Defining a scene

A scene is action. A scene happens. It is not a lengthy explanation of what happened. Or what will happen. Or even a big stretch of internal dialogue. It's not wonderfully evocative description or exposition or backstory.

So what is a scene exactly? It's "...a unit of conflict, of struggle, lived through by character and reader." (Dwight Swain, *Techniques Of the Selling Writer*)

Notice that Swain's definition of scene is not simply a moment of conflict lived through by the character alone. The reader must also experience the conflict, which means you have to bring a scene to life. A scene needs to push your character forward while dragging your reader along.

Scenes are immediate, urgent. Take a look at the examples below. Which one is a scene?

> Rachel shut her eyes and willed the fear away. She had no choice. Turning back simply wasn't an option. Turning back would take more guts than finishing it. She inched forward until her toes hung

over the edge. All that remained was one last terrifying step.

As she took the leap into nothing, Rachel began to recite the only prayer she could remember. "Give us this day our daily bread and lead us not...oh, my *Gawd!*"

She didn't stop screaming until she hit the water.

Falling back against the bed, Rachel held her arms in front of her face and fanned out the five crisp twenty dollar bills. She was a hundred bucks richer, and all she'd had to do was jump off the equivalent of a three story building into the university's diving well. No one believed she'd do it.

She hadn't been sure herself until she started climbing. The ladder had seemed to go on forever, and from the first step onto the fiberglass plank, the board wobbled right along with her nerve. Windy gusts hadn't done much for her confidence either.

But she'd done it, and now she had the money. Unable to stop grinning, Rachel silently repeated the only prayer she knew. *Give us this day our daily bread....*

The first example is part of a scene. Something is *happening.* We are *in* the moment with Rachel. In the second example, the moment of conflict is in the past. Rachel's struggle is in the past. She's simply reminiscing and congratulating herself. There is no forward movement of the plot in the second example.

Making a scene

A scene should do at least ***one*** of the following:

1. Dramatically illustrate a character's progress toward the goal or provide an experience which changes the character's goal.

2. Bring a character into conflict with opposing forces.

3. Provide a character with an experience that strengthens his motivation or changes his motivation.

A scene can do all three of those things simultaneously, **but** a scene should accomplish at least one of the above. Take your pick: G, M, or C. If a scene does none of these, why is the scene in your book? What purpose does it serve?

Rule of Thumb: Three reasons for a scene

While I'm on the subject of justifying a scene's inclusion in your book, let me add that any scene should have at least three reasons for being in your book. As already established *one of those three reasons* has to be goal, motivation, or conflict. The other two reasons for the scene can be anything you want. Here's a list of some common reasons to include a scene in a book:

introduce suspect
discover clues

sexual tension
comic relief
foreshadowing
reveal secrets
speed the pacing
establish trust between characters
betray trust between characters
The list goes on...and on...

Writers are individuals. Books are unique. That's why it's impossible to produce a complete or even comprehensive list of reasons for writing scenes. You can't "paint by numbers" when you're trying to write a book.

All you need remember is that you should have three reasons for every scene in your book. One of those reasons will be goal, motivation, or conflict. The other two reasons are up to you.

When your critique group or partner looks at you and asks, "What's the point of this scene?" and if you can't provide three solid reasons for that scene, you've got work to do. Most scenes can be strengthened. Unfortunately some need to be sacrificed. Only you can decide which must be done.

To give you an example of a hardworking scene from *The Wizard of Oz*. Think back to the apple tree scene. Dorothy and the Scarecrow discover the apple trees, but the trees are mean and stingy, refusing to let them pick apples.

This scene works on many levels. I'll take them one at a time and look at not only the reason, but how this is shown in the scene.

1. *Nurturing the main conflict*

   You see the Witch behind a tree, watching them. So

the scene serves as our warning that the Witch is not an honorable villain.

2. *Scene conflict*
   The trees slap them and throw apples. Dorothy must struggle against the trees.

3. *Characterization and foreshadowing*
   The Scarecrow, who is supposed to be as dumb as a post, has the bright idea to make faces at the trees. The trees retaliate by throwing apples. So, maybe the Scarecrow isn't as dumb as he thinks he is. This information is foreshadowing for the plan the Scarecrow hatches to free Dorothy from the Witch's castle.

4. *Opportunity to introduce new character*
   Dorothy discovers the Tinman as they rummage for apples on the ground. His discovery adds another needy member to their merry band, and they're off to see the Wizard again. They all have strong reasons for seeing the Wizard. Dorothy's sub-goal of seeing the Wizard begins to grow—like a snowball rolling downhill. It becomes more urgent, more important because additional hopes are being pinned on the promise of an unknown Wizard's skill.

5. *Strengthen Dorothy's motivation to get home*
   Back home in Kansas, the trees aren't mean and they certainly don't slap you or throw apples at you. Dorothy's unpleasant experience reminds her that she doesn't belong in Oz and strengthens her

motivation to get home. Where she understands the rules.

6. *Provide opportunity for comedy*
   From the Scarecrow's antics to the apple fight, this is a cute scene that always gets a chuckle out of the kids in the audience.

Who would have thought such an unimportant scene would be so crucial to the development of the plot? The screenplay writer. This scene is a nice piece of *work.* It was designed to do these things.

There is no limit to the number of reasons you may have for including a scene in your book. However, having ***at least*** three reasons assures you that your scenes are meaty.

Turning points in your novel

Almost without exception the turning points of your novel will be scenes. This is why evaluation of your concept and GMC is so critical in the "pre-writing" stage. Scenes build on one another.

Your character takes action (a scene). There's a reaction from the opposition, which forces the character to make another choice and take action again. Which then causes another reaction.... It's a vicious circle. And this is how it should be.

When you're planning a book, think about the middle of the book too, not just the beginning and the ending. Look at your GMC and ask yourself what kind of lesson your hero has to learn. And what kinds of scenes will give him the experience he'll need to draw upon when your book reaches the climax. Look at your GMC chart and play, "I need this." Let your mind fill with scenes that beg to be written.

In the movie *Ladyhawke* the character Navarr's goal is to kill the Bishop because Navarr wants revenge. The Bishop placed a curse on Navarr and his lover, a woman the Bishop coveted. Navarr and his love, Isabeau, are cursed to be "always together and eternally apart." He is a wolf at night, and she is a hawk by day.

Internally Navarr wants to regain the honor that he lost when he couldn't protect Isabeau from the wrath of the Bishop. Honor is of supreme importance to Navarr. His idea of honor is tangled up with the ideas of valor, a sword, and revenge. He must learn that honor isn't the sword you carry in your hand, but rather the faith you carry in your heart.

Knowing what he must learn, the writer knows that Navarr's heritage of honor—the sword waiting for the jewel stone of his generation—must be lost. A turning point for Navarr will be the loss of the physical symbol of his honor. We have to strip him bare, take away his crutch. We have an inkling of a scene that must be written. We also know that the sword as symbol must be explained. Scene number two, which must precede the loss of the sword. See how this works?

Isabeau, his lady love, wants nothing more than to survive the night and protect the wolf. These are dangerous times for a woman alone, and the danger increases as Navarr carries her back to Acquilla to face the Bishop again. Internally she just wants to hold on long enough to break the curse because that's the only way they can be together again but Navarr won't consider asking the help of the priest, who inadvertently betrayed their love in a confession to the Bishop.

Knowing that the priest will play a key role, that he can help break the curse, we know we have to find a way to force Navarr to seek the priest's help. What would it take? Gee, let's injure

Isabeau, while she's a hawk, so that the only safe place he can take her, the only other person who knows their secret, is the priest. So we have to devise a scene in which the hawk is in mortal danger.

What Isabeau needs to learn is that "Just staying alive isn't living." What scenes can we devise that will encourage her to take the risk of facing the Bishop, not for revenge, but for a chance to break the curse? How can we convince Navarr to drop his plan and trust the priest?

A complete chart on *Ladyhawke's* GMC is in the section on charts.

In your own GMC, continue to ask yourself, how can I show this? What do I need? Worry about the right order of the scenes *after* you brainstorm.

Walking away

After reviewing a number of GMC charts, you'll realize some ideas simply aren't suitable for development into novels. Take this idea for instance.

> *A woman, who is allergic to milk (conflict), searches for the perfect milk shake (goal) because she is certain that the perfect milk shake will cure her allergy (motivation).*

This idea is going nowhere. There aren't enough meaty scenes that can be developed from this GMC. Remember that the external GMC is the road map. Knowing what we know about GMC and the importance of scenes, a judgment call can be made quickly. Perhaps this idea would go in the file for short story ideas. Personally, I would relegate this idea to the round file I keep on the floor beside my desk.

Scenes and character growth

Never forget that conflict tests your characters. Otherwise, what's the point?

The Wizard of Oz contains three secondary characters that are memorable—the Scarecrow, the Tinman, and the Cowardly Lion. The reason these characters loom so large in our memories is not because they were cute and colorful and unique. It's because they grew, and we cared about them.

Think of the scene outside the Witch's castle in which the three are huddled among the rocks. The Scarecrow has to come up with a plan. He has to believe in himself, and he has to make the others believe in him. The Tinman has to get a grip on himself, a grip on the emotions he's not even supposed to have. He cares more about helping Dorothy than being upset. The Cowardly Lion has to find the courage to go with them into the castle, into certain death. The Lion has to put someone else's safety above his own. He has to trust his companions.

All three of these characters change. They are given a situation in which they must act. They go after Dorothy because they care about her. We care about them because Dorothy cares about them, and *we* care about Dorothy. We've cared about her from the beginning because we understand her GMC.

Cowards and courage do make great heroes.

Do unto others...

None of this should be obvious, by the way. Your job is to incorporate all these elements in your work and produce a seamless manuscript. The reader *shouldn't* notice how hard you work to give them multi-layered characters and a rich satisfying plot. You probably haven't noticed these elements in your own reading.

But GMC is there. Lurking at the edge of your consciousness as you read. Anchoring your belief in the story.

Go back to your keeper bookshelf. Pull down the books you really loved, the ones that have stayed with you for years. Analyze those books. Chart them. Pick them apart. Do those scenes hold up?

Show don't tell.

If you're an experienced writer, chances are you have heard the above phrase until it is tattooed on your soul. If you're a new writer, memorize it now. Show don't tell. This piece of advice is the training manual for writing scenes.

Read a few script writing or screenplay books. Rent movies and study them. Films are the pinnacle of "show don't tell." They have no choice. Movies can't "tell" you anything. Unless a voice over with a narrator is used, and have you ever noticed how that distances you from the movie? Anytime you place a layer between the reader/viewer and the scene, you are distancing that reader. You are taking one step away from that precise moment in time. You're reminding the reader that it isn't really happening right now.

You're sabotaging the reader-character bond.

Movies rarely use narrators. If a movie can't show you...if you can't understand what the movie is about by living through the character's experiences as they unfold on screen...the movie hasn't done it's job. Learn how to show the reader. Study movies. Study screenplays. Learn how they deliver backstory through characterization and dialogue. Learn how to bond your reader to your characters in the same way a movie bonds the audience to the hero.

Best example of show don't tell

Robert Newton Peck wrote a book called *Fiction is Folks—How To Create Unforgettable Characters.* The whole book is filled with examples written by Peck to illustrate his points on character. He delivers perhaps the best example of "show don't tell." All he needed was one scrap of dialogue. He didn't need to drone on with backstory or bore us with set up. Nope. Just one bit of dialogue does the trick.

Peck introduces us to an ancient Irish king—King Grady, and lets us know that King Grady is the fella that said, "What's mine is mine. And what's yours is...up for grabs."

Instant conflict!

With this statement he's already started an entire book. The goal could be anything: steal land, money, wife, horse, or a kingdom. The motivation for Grady could also be anything: greed, revenge, jealousy, defense, you name it. The conflict is clear: *the other person doesn't want to lose.*

We don't know everything about Grady, and it doesn't matter. We know that trouble has arrived in River City. This sentence jump-starts the book by throwing the character immediately into conflict. We're on the edge of our seats wondering what's going to happen. Peck has shown us a moment in time so clearly that we know there will be consequences, action, and reaction.

Using very little page space, Peck illustrates what you have to be able to do with GMC. You can't write a first chapter stuffed with backstory and flashback. You need a scene. You want your characters taking action. Use the show don't tell format.

The challenge

I've got an assignment for you—an assignment I have also done and will share after I explain the guidelines of the exercise.

1. Take ten to fifteen minutes to work up a GMC on one character. Create a completely new character and do *not* use the story you are currently working on.

2. Write a scene. Allow yourself one hour to show GMC and get the book started. The trick is to do this in the shortest amount of page space possible. SHOW DON'T TELL. And don't put more time into this exercise than one hour.

3. The only unbreakable rule: Somewhere in the scene, your character must utter the phrase, "What's mine is mine, what's yours is up for grabs."

When you work on your opening scene keep these things in mind. You need an event or circumstance. You'll need to weave in some character backstory, but don't drop in huge chunks. Give the character a goal and an opponent. Bring your character to a moment of choice. Think motivation.

In tackling this exercise, some five years ago, I chose to write an historical scene since I write contemporaries. It's much easier to create when you remove the editor who sits on your shoulder. Allow yourself to fail. Do not use the book that is near and dear to your heart for this exercise. Use something completely new, one-hundred and eighty degrees from what you're working on now.

You'll be surprised. You won't fail.

Writing about the past instead of the present gave me some extra freedom. If you write science fiction, try a thriller. If you write mystery, try a romance. If you write historical, come forward in time. I can't stress this enough. Try something new.

I had to deliver the beginnings of GMC in the shortest space possible. I managed to do it in less than two manuscript pages. What you are about to read has never been changed. This is the original piece I wrote five years ago. No editing, no fritzing around with it. (And I am still including it in this book.) People who've heard my workshop on GMC over the years will recognize it.

Since I didn't want to waste time, I even named my character King Grady. As you read, look for the GMC, both internal and external. Both are blended in this piece, as they should be in all manuscripts. There should be no obvious road signs to readers that flash, "Warning! GMC ahead."

"Sire!" blurted the page as he burst into the royal bed chamber. Belatedly, he remembered his peril, skidded to a halt, and continued in a calmer voice. "Sire, I have news."

Without turning from the basin, King Grady finished splashing his face with water and held out his ruined hand for a towel. The young king had long since grown accustomed to the sight of his misshapen hand and the two missing fingers. He no longer bothered to hide the damage done to him by an assassin's sword.

"Is this news worth your life, boy?" Grady asked as he flung the towel to the stone beneath his feet and took his sword from the attendant.

"Your Lord Councilor sent me with news from the North." The page flicked an anxious glance toward the silver blade. "He said I was to run, sir. He gave me his seal to pass the guards."

King Grady raised a brow, and his strong hand unconsciously sought the comfort of his sword hilt. He knew more of war than diplomacy. "Tell me. What Northern treachery has stirred my Lord Councilor so?"

"Duncan is dead, and Prince Corwin now sits upon the throne."

Grady stared at the page, not trusting himself to speak. Duncan had collected kingdoms in much the same way a man collected horses or a woman collected gold trinkets. And now he was dead. His death wasn't enough to purge the need for revenge from Grady's soul. Memories of his own father's blood and an assassin's ambush filled him with rage.

"Finally dead," Grady murmured, his voice cold. "Did Prince Corwin send a messenger?"

"Yes, Sire."

"Bring him to me."

"And what of the Lord Councilor?" asked the page as he backed from the room.

"What of him? Bring me the messenger."

Grady waved his attendants away and waited patiently. Duncan might be dead, but the game was not finished. Not as long as Duncan's son sat on the throne. Grady studied his maimed hand and thought of Duncan's son. He smiled grimly. Prince Corwin should have finished the job when he'd had the chance.

A commotion outside his door brought his head up, and the messenger entered the room. Without preamble, Grady asked, "Did Corwin send you?"

The messenger made an elegant bow and pulled a ribbon-tied scroll from his pouch. "Prince—King Corwin mourns his father. It was the Princess Aislinn bade me seek you and give you this."

Grady made no move to take the scroll. Instead, he leveled an intent gaze at the messenger and said, "Send Aislinn my sorrow, but tell Corwin this— From this day forth, what's mine is mine. What's his...is up for grabs."

So there you have it. The beginning of something with GMC. Obviously, the Princess Aislinn is about to offer herself in marriage to head off the train she sees coming. She knows that it's going to be a fight to the death now that Grady and Corwin are on the same level.

Do the exercise. Allow yourself the opportunity to fail. This does not have to be perfect. I wrote Grady's piece a long time ago, and I've been brave enough (forced/coerced) to share it. You don't have to show your sample to anyone. But try your hand at the exercise as a learning experience.

The purpose of the exercise is to utilize GMC, not to see how well you can write. This is about getting the meat and guts of your book on the page.

GMC for fun

After all the talk about the importance of scenes and the need to create strong GMC, your brain is probably stuck in a serious mode. Get unstuck. Play with GMC as you're learning the concept.

The most creative example of "playing" with GMC was sent to me by a student from one of my university classes. The GMC came to me as a birthday card. The GMC chart was on the front of the wonderful hand-drawn card.

	EXTERNAL	INTERNAL
Goal	Wish you a happy birthday	Find out your age
Motivation	Desire to send you best wishes	Hope you are older than me
Conflict	No stamp	You probably won't tell your age

Wrapping up

Keep in mind that you don't have to throw out everything you've written just because you didn't know or think about GMC when you wrote the manuscript. Don't throw the baby out with the bath water. Go back. Deepen the GMC whenever possible. Look for lost opportunities. Sharpen scenes to focus on your character's progress toward the goal.

Because once you've decided on GMC, all that remains is illustrating it for the reader.

1. Fiction relies heavily on scenes as does strong GMC. Narrative, exposition, and internal monologue, while also necessary, cannot replace scenes.

2. A scene is action. It's immediate. Scenes move the plot forward.

3. A scene should do at least ***one*** of the following:

    Dramatically illustrate a character's progress toward the goal or provide an experience which changes the character's goal.

    Bring a character into conflict with opposing forces.

    Provide a character with an experience that strengthens his motivation or changes his motivation.

3. You should have three reasons for every scene. One of those reasons must be goal, motivation, or conflict.

4. When planning a book, consider whether your GMC suggests scenes from the beginning, middle, and end. The middle of a book usually provides the protagonist with experiences that he will need to resolve the ultimate conflict.

5. Conflicts test your characters.

6. Analyze and chart published books. Find out how they are constructed.

7. Study movies and script writing books. Movies take the advice "show don't tell" to the max.

8. GMC can be used as a guide for revision.

Chapter Nine

GMC BRAINSTORMING

To give you a feel, as much as possible for how to create a character's GMC by brainstorming, below you'll find a transcript of a workshop session. The workshop participants selected a contemporary setting (actually more Vietnam era) and a male protagonist. As much as possible, I've tried to be true to the actual tape, but have left out sections that could be summarized more easily than shown in ping-pong dialogue style.

Imagine a large chart being filled out as the brainstorming session progressed.

DEBRA: I need to know his dominant impression. Who are we writing about? A mountain climber? Are we writing about a policeman? A bookkeeper? An ex-navy SEAL? Who are we writing—

PARTICIPANTS: Fire fighter, construction worker, military people, ex-Olympic athlete, ex-cop, ex-forest ranger...

DEBRA: We need a consensus. We've pretty much decided on "ex." He's an ex-somebody or other. Who wants him to be a military/cop/detective/dangerous protector kind of person?

PARTICIPANTS: *general agreement*

DEBRA: Okay, we've narrowed the field some. What do we want to do? Ex-military or ex-cop? Let's make it easy.

PARTICIPANTS: Ex-military.

DEBRA: What's our impression of him? Is he guarded? Is he cocky? Is he gung-ho?

PARTICIPANTS: Insecure. Wounded. Disillusioned. Dynamic. Angry. Bitter. Rigid.

DEBRA: Okay. I've got three that I like. How about bitter, disillusioned, or wounded.

PARTICIPANTS: Disillusioned.

DEBRA: We basically have disillusioned ex-military. Okay. Let's give him a name. We don't have all day here.

PARTICIPANT: Hank.

DEBRA: Okay. Fine. He's Hank. What does Hank want?

PARTICIPANT: Vacation.

DEBRA: What? Hank wants a vacation? Wait a minute now. This is not important enough for him to act against his own best interest.

PARTICIPANTS: A Swiss bank account. A job. Revenge.

DEBRA: He wants revenge?

PARTICIPANT: To be vindicated.

DEBRA: Okay. I've got no problem with that but you've slipped right over to the internal emotional element. Which is great. But let's get an external goal first.

PARTICIPANTS: Job. Money.

DEBRA: So he wants a job? So he's looking for employment? Let's stop and think for a minute. These are great things and don't stop yelling them out because we need to work through them. Is a job urgent? Can we make it urgent? Think about that. Is it exciting? Can we pull the reader in?

PARTICIPANTS: *pandemonium as the issue is hotly discussed*

DEBRA: Okay, someone said something about he wants a job because of a dishonorable discharge and it will be hard to get a job.

PARTICIPANT: He wants to get his children out of Vietnam because their mother has died.

DEBRA: Okay...so he wants to get his children out of Vietnam. No. No. That's motivation. This happens all the time. Use sticky notes so you can move things around on your chart. He wants a job.

PARTICIPANT: He wants a specific job.

DEBRA: We'll assume that we'll find an urgent job for our character, and why does he want it? So he has the money and the means to get his children out of Vietnam. Maybe he needs a job with contacts.

PARTICIPANTS: A job that will allow him to travel over there. A job that will involve him in espionage.

DEBRA: Keep in mind that those of you who are thinking, "Well, I don't really like this." That's the whole purpose. This is teaching you how to use GMC, not to send you home to write this book. You're never going to want to write someone else's GMC. This is just teaching us how to put it together. So now we need a conflict. Why can't he get a job that will allow him to get his children out of Vietnam? What's the problem?

PARTICIPANTS: Dishonorable discharge.

DEBRA: Okay. His paper's bad.

PARTICIPANT: That's why he's disillusioned.

DEBRA: Very good. We're back to why he's disillusioned.

PARTICIPANT: He has to get his children out because there's going to be some conflict, battle, or war or something.

DEBRA: Good. We've given Hank a time limit. Just thinking this through...I'm thinking here...I've got the goal as he wants to get a job. But the real goal, the bottom line, is that he wants to get his children out. That's the goal. That's urgent. That's important. He will act against his own best interest to get his children out. I think we need to fix the chart. He needs to get his children out because they are in danger. The conflict is that he has no means or way to get there.

Then I think we'd flip and put the whole discharge/disillusionment issue on the internal side. This plays to his emotions. How does he feel about the discharge, etc. he also may want to vindicate himself because emotionally he needs that vindication. He needs to feel as though he didn't fail. That he didn't deserve the discharge. Something like that.

If we were writing this book for real, we would know the details of the discharge and the exact nature of the danger to the children. But we're just using shorthand for this workshop.

PARTICIPANT: Well, where's the woman? I thought this was a romance?

DEBRA: You begin with whichever character appeals to you the most. And then you see the situation you've put them in. You have an idea of the types of people they will come in contact with. Or you already have an idea of who your heroine will be before you start working on GMC. Remember, their reason for being in your book is NOT to fall in love. Everyone has their own agenda. This will be the worst possible time for either of them to meet their soul mate. They don't have time. It's dangerous. They don't trust, whatever. So you put them into conflict. You put them in situations that throw them together, but they both have their own agenda. Things they must do.

That's why I like to work with each character separately. Complete them. See how they mesh together and then make more changes based on what I see. The changes are to increase the conflict. That was a great question, by the way.

Okay, back to Hank. Does everyone see how we have a plot going in the external GMC? Yes, getting his kids back is emotional, but doing it is physical. He's got to go somewhere and do something. Right now. It's a plot.

Now, let's look at some internal stuff. What does he have to learn? Which of you said vindicating himself? We need to know that as we work with the emotional elements.

PARTICIPANT: It's more important to be true to yourself than to be true to someone else's ideas.

DEBRA: Ooh, I like that. Your internal beliefs are more important. You shouldn't superimpose someone else's system of moral beliefs over what you know to be right and true. You can say this fifty different ways. Say it in a way that is meaningful to you so that you can use it. If you understand the phrase, then you know exactly what your character must learn.

What is Hank's inner goal? What does he want emotionally?

PARTICIPANTS: Peace. Feel vindicated. Clear his name. The love of his children. Family.

DEBRA: Okay. Someone said, "love of his children." We've gotten fifteen different answers and they're all great. We're all writing different books here, but that's all right.

He just got tossed out of the army and lost what he thought was his family. Many people feel as though the military is their family. Does he want his family back?

PARTICIPANTS: He's building a new family. Wants to be needed. Wants to be an example to his kids. He wants to be able to save his children because he couldn't save their mother.

DEBRA: He wants to be worthy then? Worthy of his children's love. He's insecure, disillusioned because of the discharge. Maybe he doesn't feel like he's worthy. All those good things.

Why does he want to feel worthy?

PARTICIPANT: Who's been taking care of these children? What are these children going to think when they see him? How many years has it been?

DEBRA: He wants to feel worthy because he hasn't done what he should have done. He didn't get them out when he should have. When he had the chance. He let other people's belief systems guide his decision. "The children are Vietnamese. They belong in their country. With their culture. They shouldn't come back to this country."

The motivation is he wants to be worthy because he hasn't done the right thing yet. And keep in mind that you do not have to agree with what we are writing on the chart. We are picking and choosing. There is no right or wrong way to do this. Each *individual's* book would probably be a million times better than what we are picking for our chart so we can keep the session moving.

No one will ever write your characters the

way you will write them, and they are the most important things in your book. In fact, I never worry about discussing my ideas because my characters are mine. They are unique. No one else can create them. Face it. There are no new plots. Another writer will never write my characters, and I'm never going to write theirs.

What's the conflict to feeling worthy?

PARTICIPANTS: He's been out of the army twenty years and he doesn't know who to go to.

DEBRA: We need something emotional. What's within himself that's keeping him from feeling worthy?

PARTICIPANT: Guilt.

DEBRA: There you go! He has to get rid of the guilt first. And to get rid of the guilt, he has to do what? He has to make it right. He has to be true to his own belief system, and then we're right back up to what he needs to learn.

GMC feeds on itself.

Charting Hank

Below you'll find Hank's chart including his tag lines and dominant impression. Remember that this chart resulted from a group brainstorming effort.

Hank needs to learn that it is important to be true to your own moral compass of right and wrong.

Never superimpose someone else's belief system over your own.

Hank disillusioned ex-military	EXTERNAL	INTERNAL
Goal	To get his children out of Vietnam	He wants to feel worthy.
Motivation	They're in danger.	He didn't do the right thing for his children because he let other people tell him what was right.
Conflict	He doesn't have the means or a way to get there.	Guilt

Chapter Ten

TWENTY-FIVE WORDS OR LESS

Using GMC is a way to wrap your brain around what the book is ***really*** about. That's what you sell to an editor. Concept and destination. GMC gives you that.

Regardless of whether you keep your GMC in your head, on notebook paper, or on a chart, you should always be able to condense the GMC into a concise statement. On demand.

A tornado blows Dorothy to Oz where she must fight a witch and seek the wizard who has the power to send her home.

You should be able to compose a short query letter that gets to the heart of your plot. You should be able to sit across from an editor at a conference and speak intelligently about your book. You achieve this brief statement of your book by working with your GMC chart and putting your plot into sentence form. Then you memorize it.

This is called "Twenty-five words or less."

What's a query letter?

If you want an editor or agent to consider your manuscript, you send them a professional invitation to read your work. This simple business letter is commonly referred to as a "query letter" and can be divided into four sections.

Salutation
Credentials
Twenty-five-words-or-less
Closing

The most important pieces of information in a query letter are a statement that the book is *finished* (usually in the opening or closing) and the paragraph containing your twenty-five-words-or-less. Editors are interested in completed manuscripts with compelling characters. To get your foot in the door, you have one—maybe two—pages to entice the editor or agent to take a chance.

You can't ramble. Your query letter is the editor's first impression of you. What do you want that dominant impression to be? Bumbling idiot? Incoherent amateur? Or would you prefer to be thought of as a skilled writer? Right. *Skilled writer* offers you the best chance to have your work read.

The four elements of a professional query each address a particular need of editors and agents. Remember...you are structuring your query to meet their needs. You want to make it easy for editors and agents to say yes. You want to give them the information they need to make a decision quickly. You're trying to sell them on your idea. Let your manuscript sell them on your actual writing ability.

Pleasant, personal ***salutation*** *such as, "Dear Ms. Smith:"*
Always use a name. Triple check the spelling and make sure your source is current. Editors play leap frog between publishing houses on a regular basis.

Introductory paragraph that establishes ***credentials***
State the kind of book, if it has won any honors, and if it's finished. In letters to agents, if you are targeting a particular publisher or genre imprint, you should include that information.

1 - 3 paragraph ***GMC summary*** *of your book covering who, what, why, and why not.*
Strive to condense the summary. Think nouns and verbs. Tell what *happens.* Be concise. Be clear. Explain the conflict. Characters and conflict are the most important elements.

Closing
Thank you for your time. I look forward to hearing from you.

Sample Letter

The twenty-five-words-or-less synopsis in the example is a mini-synopsis of one of my published novels. While the actual synopsis in the letter is more than twenty-five words, you should be able to find the GMC sentence that could stand alone. (A character wants a goal because she is motivated but she faces conflict.)

The credentials paragraph shows a typical opening

paragraph from an unpublished writer. Don't include a long list of contest wins even if you have them. Use only wins and placements in respected national contests. Editors are looking for potential, not blue ribbons.

Ms. Edith Editor
Great Books Publishing
123 Street
New York, NY 10012

Dear Ms. Editor:

I am a reader of the ABC romance line published by Great Books, and I enjoyed hearing you speak at the Memphis conference. My manuscript, *Mountain Mystic,* was a finalist in the Deep South First Chapters contest, and I feel it would be right for your line.

In *Mountain Mystic*, a contemporary midwife must begin a practice in the rural Appalachian mountain communities which financed her education. The hero is a psychic archaeologist who has come home to escape the people who want to use him and to escape the emotional echoes that haunt him.

The midwife wants the hero's help as a guide because he can ease her transition into the community, but he's a recluse who doesn't trust outsiders. Especially people who want to use him. As they fall in love, the hero must struggle with the fact that he cannot sense the heroine's emotions. She is closed to him. Loving her will mean he must take a blind leap of faith, which is something he's never had to do.

The manuscript is completed and available on request.

Sincerely,

A handle and the use of character names in query letters

You need a one sentence handle that will "place" the editor into your story world. My handle? "...a contemporary midwife must begin a practice in the rural Appalachian mountain communities which financed her education." I've given the editor my story's setting, character occupation, and motivation for moving to rural Appalachia.

Notice I did not use a proper name when referring to my character. I used an adjective and descriptive noun to create a sense of character. I used the dominant impression penciled onto my GMC chart.

Did you spot the GMC sentence? *The midwife wants the hero's help as a guide because he can ease her transition into the community, but he's a recluse who doesn't trust outsiders.* Notice the trigger words "because" and "but." The total is twenty-six words.

Another version of the *Mountain Mystic* mini-synopsis

This version, written before I had refined my techniques using GMC, is the actual three paragraph summary I used to sell this book to my editor.

> Joshua Logan has come home to the Appalachian Mountains, to the people who have always accepted him as he is without fear, without curiosity, and who have never treated him like a prized laboratory specimen. He's come home to find his balance and reassure himself that his special "gift" is not a curse,

that his strong healing touch and his uncanny ability to "read" the private minds of the people around him do not make him a freak.

Victoria Bennett owes three years of service to the cluster of rural mountain communities who paid for her medical education as a nurse and midwife specialist. To Victoria, the trade off is more than fair, because it enables her to study folk medicine first hand and to do what she has wanted to do more than anything—bring babies into the world.

Modern health care and mountain tradition clash almost before she unpacks her suitcases. She finds that being "born on the mountain" would have been a lot more helpful in establishing patient trust than six years of education. Joshua Logan, the one man who could give her the seal of approval, doesn't much like outsiders. Especially outsiders with medical training who want to study him and his grandmother's folk medicine remedies.

How do you know what's important to tell and how to organize those points?

The important information is already organized for you on your GMC chart. You simply have to decide how to convey this information in the letter. Which character is stronger? Which character will appeal more to a reader? Is it best to start with concept? What should you leave out?

Your personal style will determine how you construct your mini-synopsis. You'll notice that the two drafts of the *Mountain Mystic* synopsis are as different in tone as in structure yet both convey essentially the same information. Experiment. Get your summary down on paper. Check to be sure you've covered all the elements on your GMC chart.

Then start cutting. Cut to the bone. Don't waste a single word or a single second of the editor's time.

Wrapping up

GMC can do more for a writer than keep a book on track. GMC can help you query agents and editors with a sharp focused mini-synopsis of your story.

1. A query letter is a professional invitation to read your work.

2. Four elements of a query letter:
   Salutation
   Credentials
   Summary
   Closing

3. A one sentence "handle" sets the book in the editor's mind.

4. Use the dominant character impression instead of proper names in the query letter.

Chapter Eleven

THIS AND THAT

Can you tell it and sell it?

In addition to the voluminous questions you must ask yourself about GMC, you should also seriously consider whether you can tell and sell this story.

Is it your story to tell? Do you understand the subject matter? Can you convey the emotion your story will require? Can you handle the technical aspects of your story, if this is a techno thriller? Be honest with yourself. Sometimes it's better to put a book away and come back to the idea when you can do it justice.

Next— Can you sell it? Is there a market for your story? Is there a publisher for your erotic circus cozy mystery or a romance about two homeless people? Sometimes stories like these are hard to sell as a first book. That same idea can work beautifully as a second, third, or fourth book. If you have no market for a book, and your goal is to become published in commercial fiction, put the idea away.

No. I am not suggesting that you write only to the market. That's impossible. The trends you see now were bought eighteen months ago. Your ideas need to be fresh. You can't be Michael Crichton. That position is already filled. You can, however, be Michael Crichton with something extra.

What I'm suggesting is honesty once again. If you want to write a book that has no clear market, no one can fault you for that. Write the book. Write an incredible book. But write it knowing that you're writing a tough sell because marketing will have no idea what to do with your alien baby superheroes. And that's okay. You may sell it to the first publisher you send it to and create an entirely new genre for commercial fiction. Then again you may get forty-seven rejections.

Regardless of what you write, believe in yourself. This is a hard business. Sometimes your enthusiasm, your own belief in your talent is all the support you'll have.

Keeping the excitement going

Having considered the topic carefully, I decided that the issue is not how to keep our excitement, but how we kill and postpone our excitement. I don't believe that excitement steals quietly away when we aren't looking.

I think writers consciously and unconsciously shoo away excitement like a pesky house fly. I think writers forget that writing is about writing and not about publishing and accolades. We get caught up in excuses that have nothing to do with *starting* and *finishing* the story, which should be our primary goal.

Eventually we kill our enthusiasm for the project by telling ourselves, "It's just my practice book. It's not going to sell. It's not good enough. I'm not good enough. The story isn't unique. I don't have a deadline so there's no rush. I can't go forward until my critique group strokes me. Some contest judge didn't like it.

No one else thinks I can do this. I just read a circus clown detective mystery series like mine. I need a brainstorming group. Yada yada yada..."

Do you recognize yourself in these excuses?

Writing is hard enough without inventing excuses for why we can't do it. If you keep making excuses and postponing your time at the computer, you are going to put the creative part of your brain to sleep. The simple act of writing, writing anything, is the best way to "turn off" the internal editor who keeps you from exploding words onto the page.

Write everyday. Even if it's nothing more than a new paragraph. Put something on the page. Don't leave it blank.

A trick another writer once taught me is simple and effective. Don't turn off the computer when you are stuck. Brainstorm on screen. Type nonsense if you have to. Dialogue for the next scene. Descriptions. Rude comments. "And then the dinosaur ate the bad lawyer." (Hey, *Jurassic Park* had to come from somewhere.) After you've brainstormed nonsense for a few minutes, then turn off the computer.

Now you've got a spring board for tomorrow's writing. It's easier to sit down and write if the page isn't blank. It's easier to say, "What was I thinking! The dinosaur can't eat the lawyer...unless...there's a theme park! Yeah! That's it! A theme park."

I firmly believe that we all have dinosaur theme parks within us. Screaming to get out. If we'll just stop making excuses.

Going your own way

Learn to accept gifts of value from other writers, how-to books, and critiques. Not everything you read or hear will work for you, but some of it will be useful. Use it! Always listen. You never know who's going to have the secret of the universe.

Take what works and discard what doesn't. Recycle old ideas, invent new ones.

Writing is a solitary occupation—you, a chair, a computer.

You can't control the market. You can't make the editors read any faster than they already are. But you can control the writing.

So go write.

Appendix A

RECOMMENDED READING AND REFERENCE

WITHIN REACH OF YOUR COMPUTER OR WRITING AREA:

The Elements of Style Third Edition
William Strunk, Jr. and E.B. White
MacMillan Publishing Co., Publisher
(often referred to as: Strunk & White)

Hodges' Harbrace College Handbook
John C. Hodges, Mary E. Whitten, Winifred B. Horner, Suzanne S. Webb, Robert K. Miller
Harcourt Brace Jovanovich, Publisher

The Synonym Finder
J. I. Rodale
Warner Books, A Warner Communications Company, Publisher

Webster's Tenth New Collegiate Dictionary
Merriam-Webster, Inc. Publisher

CLOSE AT HAND, NO MORE THAN A FEW STEPS AWAY:

Techniques of the Selling Writer
Dwight V. Swain
University of Oklahoma Press, Publisher

Fiction is Folks, How to Create Unforgettable Characters
(out of print at the moment, try and find a copy anyway)
Robert Newton Peck
Writer's Digest Books, Publisher

Plot
Ansen Dibell
Writers Digest Books, Publisher

The Writer's Journey
Christopher Vogler
Michael Wiese Productions

The Hero With A Thousand Faces
Joseph Campbell
Princeton University Press

The Power Of Myth
Joseph Campbell with Bill Moyers
Anchor Books, Doubleday

SOMEWHERE IN YOUR HOUSE:

Linda Goodman's Love Signs
Linda Goodman
A Fawcett Columbine Book
Ballantine Books, Publisher
(This book is great for exploring what makes relationships work and what creates friction between a couple. This is a book I use when working on characterizations.)

The Dictionary of Cultural Literacy
E.D. Hirsch, Jr., Joseph F. Kett, James Trefil
Houghton Mifflin Company, Publisher
(This book helps when you're trying to make a decision about whether or not the average American will understand the myth, legend, biblical quote, science principle, or historical event you might mention in your work.)

The Timetables of Science
Alexander Hellemans, Bryan Bunch
Simon and Schuster, Inc., Publisher
(This helps not only with historical manuscripts, but also helps contemporary writers understand the events that influenced their characters early lives.)

The Timetables of History
Bernard Grun
Simon and Schuster, Inc., Publisher
(This book provides a good time line of history that is indispensable to historical and contemporary writers. Characters are shaped by the events of their lives.)

What Happened When
Gorton Carruth
Signet Reference, Penguin Group, Publisher
*(This book is similar to **Timetables of History**. The format is different. I have both books, but some writers might prefer one above the other.)*

Appendix B

GMC CHARTS

On the following pages you will find GMC charts for the main character(s) of:

WIZARD OF OZ

LADYHAWKE

CASABLANCA

THE CLIENT

Star Wars and **The Fugitive** were purposely left off this list so that you could create your own charts of movies that have been discussed in this book.

Note: Romance writers might also want to create charts for **The Truth About Cats and Dogs**, **The Cutting Edge**, **Pretty Woman**, and **Sense and Sensibility**.

THE WIZARD OF OZ

If you want to find your heart's desire, you must look within yourself. There's no place like home.

Dorothy unhappy teenager	EXTERNAL	INTERNAL
Goal	GET HOME 1 Get to Emerald City 2 See the Wizard 3 Get the broomstick	To find her heart's desire and a place with no trouble.
Motivation	AUNTIE EM IS SICK 1 The wizard is there. 2 He has the power to send her home. 3 The price for sending her home.	1 She's unhappy. 2 Trouble follows her everywhere.
Conflict	1 THE WITCH 2 The balloon lifts off without her.	She doesn't know what she wants.

Note: To help you identify Dorothy's central GMC at a glance, it has been capitalized. The "balloon lifting off" is not a sub-conflict related to the Witch, but neither is it the *central* conflict.

LADYHAWKE
Navarr

Honor isn't the sword you carry in your hand, but rather the faith you carry in your heart.

Navarr honorable knight	**EXTERNAL**	**INTERNAL**
Goal	He wants to kill the Bishop of Acquilla.	He wants to regain his honor.
Motivation	1 Revenge 2 The Bishop cursed Navarr and Isabeau to be "always together and eternally apart" to kill their love for each other.	His honor was lost when he couldn't protect Isabeau from the Bishop's curse.
Conflict	1 The Bishop is heavily guarded. 2 Navarr needs help to enter the city without arousing suspicion.	If he avenges his honor, he will kill any chance they have of breaking the curse.

LADYHAWKE
Isabeau

Just staying alive isn't living.

Isabeau loyal survivor	**EXTERNAL**	**INTERNAL**
Goal	She wants to survive the night and protect the wolf.	She wants to hold on long enough to break the curse.
Motivation	If she doesn't, she will become separated from Navarr.	If the curse isn't broken, she will never be able to talk to, or to touch the man she loves.
Conflict	The danger to her increases as she is carried closer to Acquilla.	Navarr won't accept the help of the priest who betrayed them and who has finally discovered a way to break the curse.

LADYHAWKE
Philippe Gaston

Honor even among thieves.

Philippe charming thief	**EXTERNAL**	**INTERNAL**
Goal	He wants to get as far away as possible from the dungeons and guards of Acquilla. *HE WANTS TO BRING NAVARR AND ISABEAU BACK TOGETHER.*	He wants to be honorable/respected and a part of something instead of apart from everything. (Remember the cell mate who he said "at least respected" him.
Motivation	He is a convicted thief and the sentence is death. *HE BEGINS TO CARE ABOUT NAVARR AND ISABEAU. THEIR LOVE IS HONORABLE AND TRUE, AND THEY ARE PEOPLE DESERVING OF HAPPINESS.*	1 He is uncertain of his value as a human being. 2 He is alone.
Conflict	He becomes entangled in the affairs of Navarr who wants Philippe to help him sneak into Acquilla. *NAVARR WON'T LISTEN TO THE PRIEST.*	1 He won't believe in himself or trust himself to know what is right. 2 He sees too many shades of gray in the world, and doing the honorable thing always causes him trouble. 3 He bargains with God instead of making his own choices.

Note: The change in typeface in the External GMC indicates a change in the character's original GMC. It is not merely an additional goal, but a complete change.

CASABLANCA
Rick Blaine

One person can make a difference in the world.
Women in war must make desperate choices. (Think of the newlywed.)

Rick cynical loner	EXTERNAL	INTERNAL
Goal	1 Keep bar open 2 Punish Ilsa 3 Get Ilsa and Victor on plane	1 Regain the love he had in Paris 2 To do what's right for the world
Motivation	1 Needs money and people depend on him 2 Because she left him in Paris 3 Insure her safety	1 The pain of losing Ilsa has never gone away. 2 Daily, he finally sees what the war is doing to people around him.
Conflict	1 The French Prefect has all the power. 2 Punishing her puts her in more danger. 3 Victor has been put in jail.	1 Ilsa is married. 2 He must put aside his own happiness.

CASABLANCA
Ilsa Lund-Laslow

To put the problems of the world before her own happiness.

Ilsa dutiful wife	**EXTERNAL**	**INTERNAL**
Goal	Get husband on a plane to Lisbon	To find happiness and passion again
Motivation	He's in grave danger.	1 She realizes she didn't marry Victor out of romantic love, but out of respect. 2 Love is what she had with Rick in Paris.
Conflict	Once he's safe she can stay with Rick.	1 Rick won't let her leave Victor, who needs her by his side. 2 Both men in her life are too honorable for her to make selfish choice.

THE CLIENT
Reggie Love

You rebuild trust by giving people new memories of you.
You have to find your way alone before others will follow you.

Reggie trustworthy lawyer	EXTERNAL	INTERNAL
Goal	1 Wants to take on a legendary district attorney 2 Wants to protect Mark from the government, the bad guys, and himself	1 Wants to be better than her past 2 Wants to be a part of her kids lives again
Motivation	1 To prove herself 2 Mark has no one else to help him and the wrong move will get him killed.	1 She's ashamed of the way she drank. 2 She loves and misses them.
Conflict	1 She's only been practicing for two years. 2 Mark doesn't trust her.	1 People don't forget or forgive drunks easily. 2 They don't trust her.

THE CLIENT
Mark Sway

No one can survive alone.
We all have to learn to ask for help.

Mark enterprising problem child	EXTERNAL	INTERNAL
Goal	1 Cover up his involvement in a man's suicide 2 Protect his family	He wants someone to shoulder the burden, someone he can count on to be the adult and keep him safe.
Motivation	1 He wants to keep out of trouble. 2 Threats have been made to their lives.	Mark has had to grow up fast and fend for himself as his mother works to keep a pitiful roof over their heads.
Conflict	1 The physical evidence keeps tripping up his lies. 2 He doesn't know who to trust.	He's too proud and too cool to ask for help.

INDEX

X, Y, Z

ABOUT THE AUTHOR

National bestselling and award winning author Debra Dixon has eight published novels to her credit. In addition to seeing her work published internationally, she has been awarded both the Georgia Romance Writers' "Maggie" and *A Little Romance Magazine's* ROMY for excellence in romance fiction. *Romantic Times Magazine* has nominated her twice for Career Achievement Awards. Additionally, her published books have been consistently recognized as finalists for the Colorado Award of Excellence, the Virginia Holt Medallion, and the National Readers' Choice Award for romance fiction.

In addition to speaking at numerous regional and national conferences Debra developed and continues to teach a novel writing course for the University of Memphis as well as one-day writing workshops across the country. Gryphon Books for Writers suggested she write a "how-to" book based on her most requested workshop—GMC: Goal, Motivation, and Conflict—as the first in Gryphon's *"Books for Writers"* series.

Although she has now "retired" from a successful career as a small business consultant, she continues to serve on the Board of Directors for three corporations, including an international trading company. She lives in Memphis with her husband and son.